Praise for *Communicate Like a Leader*

"If you're a micromanager, you need to know it's not ̶, ̶t̶h̶e̶ ̶m̶o̶s̶t̶ the most labor-intensive leadership style. When you read *Communicate Like a Leader*, you'll learn strategic communication skills that will improve your relationship with your people and actually make leading easier. Dianna Booher is the communication guru of the 21st century!"

—**Ken Blanchard, coauthor of *The New One Minute Manager® and *One Minute Mentoring***

"Great leaders are great communicators, as Dianna Booher points out in this smart, useful book. If you want to become a top-notch strategic communicator, you'd do well to heed the advice in its pages."

—**Marshall Goldsmith, executive coach, business educator, *New York Times* bestselling author, and Thinkers50 #1 leadership thinker in the world**

"Dianna Booher's brilliant new book, *Communicate Like a Leader*, is the single-best communication guide I have ever read. In it are thirty-six clear, concise, relevant, and practical bits of strategic advice on how to connect with others. No fluff. No wasted words. All substance. I guarantee you that there is something in this book that you can use immediately—and more that you can apply tomorrow and the next day and the next. Buy this right now, read it as soon as you get it, and then put Dianna's expert advice to work for you. You will be very glad that you did."

—**Jim Kouzes, coauthor of the bestselling *The Leadership Challenge* and Dean's Executive Fellow of Leadership, Leavey School of Business, Santa Clara University**

"Everything they didn't teach you at Harvard Business School—but should have—about leadership communication in the real world of work."

—**John Addison, bestselling author; Leadership Editor, *Success* magazine; and CEO, Addison Leadership Group**

"More than a mere treatise on communication, this is an extremely practical and actionable book about becoming a better leader. It happens that leaders do their work by communicating, and Booher provides valuable tactics to use in a wide variety of circumstances. Every reader is guaranteed to take away some useful practices."

—**Jack Zenger, CEO, Zenger Folkman, and bestselling coauthor of *The Extraordinary Leader* and *Speed***

"Dianna Booher has done it once again. This book is a must-read for anyone seeking clear, practical, and actionable advice."

—Catherine Blades, Senior Vice President, Corporate Communications, Aflac Inc.

"Great leaders have one thing in common: they are all great communicators. They have discovered how to convert their keen awareness into ideas that speak to one's emotions and ambitions. They understand that if their message does not take deep root, it will likely make little difference in shaping outcomes. In her newest book, *Communicate Like a Leader*, Dianna Booher calls upon her vast body of work to create an inspirational playbook for leaders in pursuit of excellence. A must-read for people seeking to propel their career."

—Bill Yancey, Managing Director, Operations, Hilltop Securities Inc.

"Communication and leadership are critical for all success. Dianna Booher is an expert on both fronts and an author of forty-seven books! Learn from her wisdom. Buy this book, read this book, and learn from the very best—I do!"

—Dr. Peter Legge, OBC, CSP, CPAE Hall of Fame, CEO and Chairman, Canada Wide Media Limited

COMMUNICATE LIKE A LEADER

Other Business Books by Dianna Booher

What More Can I Say? Why Communication Fails and What to Do About It

Creating Personal Presence: Look, Talk, Think, and Act Like a Leader

*Communicate With Confidence: How to Say It Right the First Time
and Every Time (Revised and Expanded Edition)*

*The Voice of Authority:
10 Communication Strategies Every Leader Needs to Know*

*Booher's Rules of Business Grammar: 101 Fast and
Easy Ways to Correct the Most Common Errors*

Your Signature Work: Creating Excellence and Influencing Others at Work

Your Signature Life: Pursuing God's Best Every Day

*From Contact to Contract: 496 Proven Sales Tips to Generate More Leads,
Close More Deals, Exceed Your Goals, and Make More Money*

Speak With Confidence: Powerful Presentations That Inform, Inspire, and Persuade

E-Writing: 21st-Century Tools for Effective Communication

Good Grief, Good Grammar

To the Letter: A Handbook of Model Letters for the Busy Executive

Great Personal Letters for Busy People

The Complete Letter Writer's Almanac

*Clean Up Your Act: Effective Ways to Organize
Paperwork and Get It Out of Your Life*

Executive's Portfolio of Model Speeches for All Occasions

The New Secretary: How to Handle People as Well as You Handle Paper

Writing for Technical Professionals

Winning Sales Letters

Get a Life Without Sacrificing Your Career

Ten Smart Moves for Women

Get Ahead, Stay Ahead

COMMUNICATE
LIKE*A LEADER

Connecting **Strategically** to Coach, Inspire, and Get Things Done

BY **DIANNA BOOHER**

* To all you strict grammarians out there: Yes, we know "like" in the book's title should be "as." But what do you want—good grammar or a good title?

Berrett–Koehler Publishers, Inc.
a BK Business book

Berrett-Koehler Publishers, Inc.
1333 Broadway, Suite 1000
Oakland, CA 94612-1921
Tel: (510) 817-2277   Fax: (510) 817-2278   www.bkconnection.com

Ordering Information
Quantity sales. Special discounts are available on quantity purchases by corporations, associations, and others. For details, contact the "Special Sales Department" at the Berrett-Koehler address above.
Individual sales. Berrett-Koehler publications are available through most bookstores. They can also be ordered directly from Berrett-Koehler: Tel: (800) 929-2929; Fax: (802) 864-7626; www.bkconnection.com
Orders for college textbook/course adoption use.
Please contact Berrett-Koehler: Tel: (800) 929-2929; Fax: (802) 864-7626.
Orders by U.S. trade bookstores and wholesalers.
Please contact Ingram Publisher Services, Tel: (800) 509-4887; Fax: (800) 838-1149; E-mail: customer.service@ingrampublisherservices.com; or visit www.ingrampublisherservices.com/Ordering for details about electronic ordering.

Berrett-Koehler and the BK logo are registered trademarks of Berrett-Koehler Publishers, Inc.

Printed in the United States of America

Berrett-Koehler books are printed on long-lasting acid-free paper. When it is available, we choose paper that has been manufactured by environmentally responsible processes. These may include using trees grown in sustainable forests, incorporating recycled paper, minimizing chlorine in bleaching, or recycling the energy produced at the paper mill.

Cataloging-in-Publication Data is available at the Library of Congress.
ISBN: 978-1-62656-900-3

First Edition
21 20 19 18 17   10 9 8 7 6 5 4 3 2 1

Cover design: The BookDesigners

Produced by Wilsted & Taylor Publishing Services
Copy editing: Melody Lacina
Design: Nancy Koerner
Composition: Sev Saffen

Contents

PART 2

STRATEGIC CONVERSATIONS
Connect With Intent

PART 3

STRATEGIC NEGOTIATIONS
Look for Mutual Opportunities

PART 4

STRATEGIC SPEAKING
Persuade Minds and Win Hearts

COMMUNICATE LIKE A LEADER

The Challenge of Leadership Communication

Without strategy, execution is aimless.
Without execution, strategy is useless.

—MORRIS CHANG,
CHINESE AND AMERICAN BUSINESSMAN,
FOUNDING CHAIRMAN OF TAIWAN SEMICONDUCTOR

Just what you don't want to find in your inbox on a Monday morning: A resignation letter from an excellent employee. No reason given and no mention of another job offer. I called Rachel in to ask for an explanation.

"I just can't take it anymore." She started to tear up.

"Take what?" I asked. She worked in another wing of our building, and I was indeed clueless about why the marketing specialist was so unhappy in her job.

"I just can't work for him anymore." I did at least know the "him" she reported to as her supervisor. "I get a big knot in my stomach every morning before I come to work. Really physically sick. My husband has been trying to get me to resign for months. July has been terrible. Wally hasn't spoken to me all month. Walks right past my desk every morning. Goes to lunch right past my desk every day. Doesn't say a word."

"I'm sorry to hear this."

"He's always angry about something he thinks I didn't do right. I never know exactly what. He just completely ignores me."

"How do you know he's angry at you?"

"Because when he is speaking, he's cross-examining me. He doesn't trust me. Every time I leave my desk for fifteen minutes, when I get back, it's, 'Where have you been?' 'Why did that take so long?' And after I hang up the phone, it's, 'Who was that?' 'What did you tell them?' I've never given him any reason *not* to trust me. He's just always looking over my shoulder, double-checking everything. And I learned to handle the client calls from listening to *him*!" She started to tear up again.

"I'm sorry. I had no idea this was happening."

Rachel had been a quick learner, picking up pointers from all our star performers in and out of the office. Consequently, she'd been able to take on more responsibility than her original job entailed.

"One day he's talking to me about his family, and my family, movies—like we're best friends. And the next day, he's treating me like I can't be trusted."

"How long has this been going on?"

"A year."

FROM BUDDY TO BULLY—UNINTENTIONALLY

"People don't leave an organization; they leave a boss" has become a truism in the workplace for good reason. Emotional instability, for whatever reason, can infect the workplace and lower productivity as surely as malfunctioning equipment. Often, the person causing the retention problem has moved from buddy to bully without intending ill will. It just "happens." That boss got promoted from supervisor to manager or from manager to senior executive without adequate leadership and communication skills for the job. As a result, the boss gets stuck in micromanagement mode.

If that person happens to be *you*, this book will help you get un-stuck. These strategic communication skills, attitudes, and mindsets separate those

- Professionals who succeed at the executive level from those who don't

- Star sales professionals breaking through barriers and exceeding quotas from those living paycheck to paycheck

- Millennials tagged as "high-potentials" from those labeled average performers

- Entrepreneurs who succeed wildly from those who barely eke out a living

The most visible difference in each of these situations is a person's ability to communicate vision, initiatives, assignments, ideas, and strategy to audiences at all levels in various settings.

Emotional instability for whatever reason can infect the workplace and lower productivity as surely as **malfunctioning equipment**.

WHAT IS STRATEGIC COMMUNICATION?

Strategic communication forms the very core of leadership. When you as a leader speak, meet, negotiate, write, or network, you either clarify or confuse, motivate or demoralize, engage or enrage employees. And they, in return, will either give 110 percent of their loyalty, support, and skill to accomplish your mission—or disengage, divert your focus, and drain your energy in dealing with them.

The dictionary defines *strategic* as "pivotal," "essential," or "relating to long-term importance to achieve a plan or goal." That's how I'll be using "strategic" going forward in this book: those messages, meetings, conversations, discussions, or presentations that have pivotal, long-term payoff versus "routine" communication.

Back to Rachel's situation. Fortunately, my company did get Rachel's situation corrected by changing her reporting relationship and getting counseling for her supervisor, and she did stay with us. But similar problems occur daily in the workforce. Such situations become a crisis for all involved for these reasons:

- Micromanaged employees work and live under undue stress that often leads to job loss—either by their choice or by termination.

- Micromanagers become less and less productive under a heavier and heavier workload because they do their own regular job—and then take on the jobs of those they supervise.

- Organizations lose some of their best employees and grow less productive and profitable because professionals who get promoted for their technical skills do not learn the strategic communication skills necessary to succeed in their new leadership role.

We'll discuss several reasons for micromanagement and how to overcome it later in the book. But for now, my point is that fewer and fewer professionals arrive at their position with all the leadership communication skills they need to master the job.

In a recent *Wall Street Journal* survey of nearly 900 executives, 92 percent said soft skills were equally or more important than technical skills. But 89 percent reported that they had a very or somewhat difficult time finding people with those attributes. And they say the problem spans all age groups and experience levels.[1]

ALWAYS TRANSLATE TO THE STRATEGIC

As Cool Hand Luke famously said in the movie by the same name, "What we've got here is a failure to communicate." To paraphrase his observation: What we have here is a failure to translate to the strategic message for groups at different levels in your organization.

For example, let's say your daughter Jordan has won first place in the school district's ninth-grade science fair, and you're proud of her research for that innovative project. You tell the grandparents about the big win, and they're thrilled as well. Assume you have a family reunion the following month with more than 100 cousins, aunts, uncles, and in-laws attending. Tell them about the same science project, and you'll probably find them less interested than Jordan's grandparents. After all, the aunts, uncles, and cousins have kids involved in science projects of their own.

Then let's assume you have an industry meeting the next week, and you tell that group about Jordan's science project. How interested will they be? And how interested will your seatmate on your cross-country flight be when you tell him about the science project? Unless you share a profound lesson learned about volunteerism or fund-raising success that applies to professional associations or to your seatmate's company, your listener will probably care a great deal *less* than the grandparents.

The further removed the link to your child, the less the listener cares about your news—and the greater skill you'll need to find a worthwhile idea to share from the science project. In other words, your ability to take an experience from one context and reapply it in a larger context to a different audience with wider interests represents strategic insight and communication.

We intuitively understand this need to translate in personal situations. But many leaders fail to "get it" in the workplace. In doing presentation coaching, I can't tell you how often managers have told me about trying to give the same presentation to several different audiences and levels of management—and failing.

STRATEGIC COMMUNICATION
VERSUS TACTICAL COMMUNICATION

Whether you're in marketing, sales, operations, finance, research, IT, legal, or human resources, tactical thinkers communicate directives to get things done. They decide who does what when. Unfortunately, the tactical things that get done may not always be the *wisest* things or the *most profitable* things with long-term payoff. Tactical thinking is critical—but common.

Still, strategic thinkers stand out from the crowd. Big-picture thinking uniquely positions you as the resource for focus, problem analysis, and innovation.

But strategic thinking puts points on the scoreboard *only if you can communicate your thinking clearly*. And the more respect your thinking earns—that is, the more visibility you get—the more often you'll need to communicate your thinking up, down, and across the organization.

This book offers help as you think and communicate strategically to fulfill your most essential responsibilities as a leader. **Its 36 brief chapters fall into six distinct categories—a suite of leadership *communication* skills.**

- People Development
  (hiring, firing, assigning, directing, coaching)

- Conversations

- Negotiations

- Speaking

- Writing

- Meetings

Why leadership communication? Because communication comprises the essence of influencing a team to accomplish a mission. The book is NOT intended to be a comprehensive, all-purpose management or leadership book. Neither does this volume focus on general interpersonal skills. My earlier book *Communicate With Confidence: How to Say It Right the First Time and Every Time* contains more than 1,200 tips to improve interpersonal communication in myriad situations at work, home, and elsewhere.

Rather, this book focuses specifically on those relationships, situations, and decisions you face because of your position and responsibility as a leader. Recall that strategic refers to something essential or pivotal for the long term. In that sense, the degree to which you can communicate strategically in every interaction will determine your ultimate success with peers, staff, clients, suppliers, and your own executive team.

Tactical thinkers get things done. Strategic thinkers get the *right* things done. Tactical communicators tell others how to get things done. Strategic communicators *lead others* to get the *right* things done. They

— Cast the vision, chart the course, and "go first" to lead the way and set the example

— Communicate up and down the chain of command and across department lines to make sure all stakeholders understand the big-picture impact

— Network strategically to connect and involve the right people for input and participation—and then negotiate for mutual benefit

— Speak persuasively, write clearly, and conduct meetings that deliver results

Consequently, strategic thinkers and communicators typically end up in the executive ranks of large organizations or build their own entrepreneurial business. Whatever your plans, strategic communication will be the smoothest, most direct route to success.

PART 1

STRATEGIC LEADERSHIP
Think Long-Term Investment in People and Payoff

Leadership is not a magnetic personality, that can just as well be a glib tongue. It is not "making friends and influencing people," that is flattery. Leadership is lifting a person's vision to higher sights, the raising of a person's performance to a higher standard, the building of a personality beyond its normal limitations.

—PETER F. DRUCKER, AUSTRIAN-BORN AMERICAN
MANAGEMENT CONSULTANT, EDUCATOR, AND AUTHOR

Leadership is a potent combination of strategy and character. But if you must be without one, be without the strategy.

—GENERAL NORMAN SCHWARZKOPF, UNITED STATES ARMY,
WHO LED ALL COALITION FORCES IN THE GULF WAR

The art of effective listening is essential to clear communication, and clear communication is necessary to management success.

—JAMES CASH PENNEY, BUSINESSMAN AND ENTREPRENEUR
WHO FOUNDED THE J. C. PENNEY RETAIL CHAIN

CHAPTER 1

Communicating as a Leader and as a Manager

The people who influence you are
the people who believe in you.

—HENRY DRUMMOND, 18TH-CENTURY
ENGLISH BANKER, AUTHOR, AND MEMBER
OF THE BRITISH PARLIAMENT

When my client Mitch visited our office, he had both good news and bad news. "Let me give you the good news first. . . . A couple of partners and I just bought a telecom at a great price—basically a spin-off of the entire division I used to manage."

"That *is* great news." I followed up with several questions and learned that the spin-off he referred to was from a nationally known company that had downsized his entire division.

"The downsizing didn't sound exactly like good news at the time," Mitch continued. "But it has turned out that way. That is, if we can make a go of this telecom venture."

"Well, I'd say you're off to a good start. Everything sounds like *good* news so far," I said.

"Right. . . . Well, here's the *bad* news: I've placed about 40 to 45 technical experts in leadership roles. Brilliant at their individual jobs—don't get me wrong. But they've had only *limited* experience as managers. At best, they were supervisors at their old jobs. . . . They have the technical know-how. But now they need to communicate with their peers in other areas, deal with customers and suppliers, and interact with the executive leaders on the new team."

I nodded, not wanting to interrupt to tell him how common his story sounded.

"They're communicating at about this level," Mitch gestured with a wave of his hand about mid-thigh, as if measuring the height of a small child, "and I need them to start thinking and communicating from this perspective." He repeated the gesture at hairline level.

Our communication consulting firm hears this complaint frequently regarding how staff members deliver executive briefings and write sales proposals.

"If I can give you these people for a few days, can you teach them what they need to know to become real leaders—not just good in their functional roles?"

Music to my ears. I always love hearing someone voice the difference between *managing* (maintaining the status quo) and *leading* (improving the status quo).

You may hire a financial advisor to "manage" your money during a great bull market. He or she may help you reorganize your investments: consolidate your accounts from two different organizations into one bank account, project your future income needs for a child's education or your own retirement, and consolidate your mutual fund investments into fewer families of funds. But after a year, if that person is not increasing the *value* of your investment portfolio, you'll probably be looking for a new financial advisor. You want someone who can *improve* the situation, not simply *maintain* it.

That distinction between leader and manager may have absolutely *nothing* to do with position or title. You can lead as a project team member, an association member, a parent, a researcher, a customer, or an assistant.

Consider the nine differences between leaders and maintainers in the following chart.

THE DIFFERENCE BETWEEN
MAINTAINERS AND LEADERS

Managers/Maintainers	Leaders
Have information, facts, or skills. They may even show mastery of a craft, job, or topic.	Have superior reasoning skills and judgment. They know how to apply their information, the facts, or their skills to a specific situation at the right time, in the right way, for the best outcome for all concerned.
Often try to lead people from the simple to the complex.	Most often try to break the complex down to the simple.
Take things apart to analyze.	Put things together to conclude and apply.
Like to do things their way. They tend to place great trust in their own expertise and control. Their thinking seems to follow the old adage: "If it ain't broke, don't fix it."	Like to get input from several trusted sources. They listen with an open mind and weigh facts and ideas before rushing to accept or reject these ideas as valid.
Know when to be abstract to avoid offense, blame, or questions.	Know when an ounce of concrete and specificity is worth a ton of abstraction.

THE DIFFERENCE BETWEEN MAINTAINERS AND LEADERS *(cont.)*

Managers/Maintainers	Leaders
Communicate directly and frequently. These communication habits ensure control of processes and people.	Communicate directly, frequently, consistently, tactfully, and compassionately. These communication habits demonstrate passion, engagement, and concern.
Practice self-discipline and *expect* their staff to do the same.	Understand *why* they practice self-discipline and *inspire* their staff to do the same.
Do things right.	Do the right things.
Always know *how* to do things.	Always know *why* to do things.

As you plan strategic communication—whether for a conversation, a briefing, a report, a meeting, or an email—keep in mind these principles: The right timing. A clear conclusion. Specific application to your audience. Simple, tactful, concerned phrasing. The *why* behind the decision or action. Inspiration. The right thing to do. We'll dig deeper into all these principles as we move further through the book.

➤ *The manager's goal:* Smooth, flawless operations.

➤ *The leader's goal:* Improve the situation. "Up" the game or performance. Increase the value or asset.

CHAPTER 2

Have a Ready Answer for THIS One Key Question —Always

Like a diaphanous nightgown, language both hides and reveals.

—KAREN ELIZABETH GORDON, AUTHOR

As a leader, you hear questions every day, some serious, some trivial. "What do you hear about the merger plans?" "Do you think our budget is going to be cut?" "Can we get an extension on the deadline?" "Are we going to have to work over the weekend?"

But the ONE question that you have to answer correctly every time is this: "What are you working on?"

It's particularly critical that you get the answer right when responding to your boss. Your reputation can also suffer when you flub that question with peers.

WHY IS THIS SO DIFFICULT?

For the most part, you and your team need to communicate details to run your project, department, or division. For that, you need charts, graphs, slides, spreadsheets, meetings, presentations, proposals, metrics, and reports. You accomplish things with these tools, and the associated data make perfect sense to you. The abbreviations, acronyms, illustrations, and other shortcuts save you time and ensure a common understanding.

So you have a tendency to try to communicate with the same tools and in that same fashion to those outside your functional area.

But don't.

That jargon, those communication tools, and that level of detail won't make sense to people on the outside. They'll likely conclude that you don't know how to synthesize, summarize, and interpret how your work contributes to the big picture of the organization.

> But the **ONE question** that you have to answer correctly every time is this: **"What are you working on?"**

Granted, habits are difficult to break. But they can hinder communication and halt your career growth.

SO HOW SHOULD YOU ANSWER THAT ONE QUESTION?

Put aside your complicated tools. Forget how much effort you've put into the project. Time spent does not equal value created. Instead, focus on these few things to answer the big question:

Part 1: We're working on solving X problem(s).

Part 2: Here's why it matters to the organization. . . .

Part 3: Here are the outcomes we're working toward. . . .

Part 4: *(Optional—depending on who asked the question)*
This is how the work may affect the budget and timeline as far as you're concerned. . . .

TIME spent does not equal **VALUE** created.

HOW DO YOU EDUCATE OTHERS
OUTSIDE YOUR FUNCTIONAL AREA?

You shouldn't and you don't.

If you do, you'll be irrelevant. While coaching sales teams on presentations or sales proposals, I frequently hear such comments as "We have to educate our customers on our product" or "Our customers really don't understand how best to use our process and the services we provide, so our real challenge is to educate them on exactly what we do."

I have to bite my tongue to keep from shouting, "How insulting to your customers!" That's like saying, "We need smarter customers." Very few customers will likely agree with you on that.

Ditto with internal customers. They don't want to be "educated" about what *you're* doing. They want *you* to be educated about what *they're* doing and then translate what *you're* doing for them. In other words, get aboard *their* train.

SO WHAT'S YOUR REAL JOB AS A
STRATEGIC THINKER AND LEADER?

Become a translator: "So what that means for you (for the organization, for our customers, for our partners, for our suppliers) is that . . ."

Sift through and analyze the metrics, data, and details needed for your functional role. Then draw some conclusions about the bigger picture: How does your work benefit them? Their budget? Their deadlines? Their costs? Their savings? Their profits? Their processes? Make their work easier? But never pass on your raw information.

Instead, communicate clearly an answer to this ONE question: "What are you working on?" And if your answer is strategic (relevant, tailored, and timely), the listener will care.

That's relevancy. And staying relevant is a leader's strategic responsibility.

CHAPTER 3

Make Sure the Team
Knows the Deliverables

*The two words "information" and "communication" are often
used interchangeably, but they signify quite different things.
Information is giving out; communication is getting through.*

—SYDNEY J. HARRIS, HUMORIST

It's not enough that you can answer the one question about what you're
"working on." Are you sure your own team knows the outcomes
they're responsible to deliver?

In survey after survey, managers report that their team understands
organizational goals and initiatives. Yet team members *themselves* say
they do not. In a recent worldwide Gallup poll among 550 organizations and 2.2 million employees, only 50 percent of employees "strongly
agreed" that they knew what was expected of them at work.[2] Obviously, there's a disconnection here.

Consider this all-too-likely scenario: A dad says to a disappointed
teen after his prom plans with friends fall through because of transportation costs, "Don't worry, son. I'll see that you have transportation to
the prom." Overhearing the conversation, the mom expects the dad to
offer their son the family Lexus. The son walks away thinking, "Great.

Dad's going to pay for a limo." On prom weekend, when his dad arranges his work schedule to be home to drive his son and his date to the prom in the family car, somebody's sure to be disappointed.

The same happens with staff at work. Expectations and outcomes don't always align. For example: The vice president expects the social marketing campaign to generate 500 inquiries on the new product within the two-week launch period. The actual outcome from the social media team's effort results in a 60 percent increase in *visits* to the company website but only 52 *inquiries* on the new product.

Leadership demands communicating a clear vision and goals, encouraging your team to collaborate on the strategic plan, and then inspiring followers to deliver specific outcomes. But let's face it: As the Gallup survey suggests, many leaders fall flat on their face when it comes to communicating the expected outcomes clearly. And the more times and the more layers of the organization that those goals need to travel through, the more chances that things get "lost in translation."

The following attitudes and practices signal danger. Consider the accompanying safeguards.

INCONSISTENCY VERSUS CONSISTENCY

Ineffective leaders fear that others will "catch them" in inconsistencies. As much as possible, these leaders stay behind closed doors.

Effective leaders say what they mean and mean what they say. They never fear that others will find a mismatch between words and action—between values they communicated in an all-hands meeting, for example, and what they're planning to do at an executive retreat. They don't have to remember what they told Rudy to make sure it "syncs" with how they told Gabriella to handle a similar issue. They practice consistency.

UNWILLINGNESS TO ADMIT MISTAKES VERSUS ACCOUNTABILITY

Leaders expect their team members to own a problem, a task, a project—to take responsibility and see it through to completion. That's why it's devastating to their own credibility and to team morale when leaders refuse to clearly communicate, "I made a mistake." "I misjudged the situation in that I should have considered X." "I didn't react appropriately." Failure to "own up" sets up a mindset for failure to deliver.

Effective leaders shoulder responsibility and accept accountability as a visible part of their role.

THE ONE-SIZE-FITS-ALL PERSPECTIVE VERSUS PERSONALIZATION

Struggling communicators plan their messages (emails, speeches, briefings, announcements, webcasts) with a one-size-fits-all mentality: to "the team," "their staff," "the company." That is, struggling leaders think of the universality of what they need to communicate; as a result, their comments become vague and general.

Effective leaders, as they communicate, consider their team of *individual performers*—not a group that acts and responds collectively. Why will Janet, Barry, Haroon, and Eduardo care about this? In what ways does the message apply specifically to how these people do their jobs? If you're encouraging your team to find ways to cut costs during the next quarter, use an example of saving $8,000 on paper supplies that Barry might identify with, along with the cost-cutting example of saving $100,000 by using temporary rather than full-time employees—an example that Janet would identify with as manager of a much larger division. These two very specific case studies would communicate to the entire team that you're familiar with how they individually contribute to the team.

Rather than babbling about diluted abstractions, strong leaders provide specifics. Their conversations, briefings, and emails are focused, practical, and relevant.

Such personalized communication elicits individual engagement and commitment—in much the same way a personal invitation to a party gets an answer and a Facebook post to a group of 80 may or may not.

WAR STORIES AND VICTORY LAPS
VERSUS HERO HIGHLIGHTS

Struggling leaders typically tell a lot of this-is-how-I-did-it war stories as they share initiatives and launch new projects. People learn from the past, of course, and you want the past to serve you well. But taking victory laps rather than forging on to the future weakens you in the eyes of your followers.

Stronger communicators more often tell this-is-how-*they*-did-it hero stories that showcase other employees' successes on the job. Consider the strategic difference in morale in making others the heroes in your stories. You've seen many companies use this approach in their TV commercials. A video highlights key employees, who relate why they became an engineer, a scientist, or a physicist at XYZ corporation. These featured employees become the "face" for the big corporation.

You can do the same as a leader to build your team members' morale. When you celebrate wins, tell *their* individual stories and contributions—not just yours and not just the stories of the collective team.

DON'T-MAKE-ME DEMEANOR VERSUS
OPEN BODY LANGUAGE

As a parent, have you ever warned your quarreling kids, "Don't make me have to come to your room to settle this"? Or maybe you remember your own parent's dire warning: "Don't make me stop this car to see what this is all about!" Or, "Don't make me send you away from the table without dinner!" All said with the appropriate scowl, tone of voice, and wagging finger.

Struggling leaders often appear to be in similar pain as they communicate a challenging new mission: negative words, nervous gestures, fatigued expression, angry tone, glaring eyes, frustrated frown, doubtful shrug, slumped shoulders, and defeated stare. All of this negative body language stands in the way of communicating clearly with your staff. Consider it a blockade to delivering anything of value—internally or externally.

By contrast, effective communicators know that their body language and behavior trump their words at this strategic time. Rather than a gloom-and-doom-delivery, their facial expression and gestures are positive, open, energetic, warm, and affirming. Their body language shows excitement about the vision and confidence in the team to deliver the desired outcome. They smile sincerely. They often ditch the desk barrier in favor of sitting side by side with the other person. If speaking to a larger group, they approach them rather than stand behind the barrier of a lectern. They extend their hands and arms, greeting others and welcoming questions rather than pulling back or standing rigidly in place as if expecting to be the target for darts.

Your "visual" counts. Check a mirror occasionally—particularly on tense days in tough situations.

INEFFECTIVE VERSUS EFFECTIVE VERIFICATION QUESTIONS

Great leaders understand the strategic importance of continually verifying that team members understand the expected outcomes for the internal or external client—annual, quarterly, or project deliverables, along with the metrics used to track performance.

So what's the *least* effective way to verify with your staff or a peer? By asking, "Do you understand?" Confident team members invariably say yes. They want to please.

But the most effective leaders *verify* for themselves strategic steps. They *test* understanding by asking thoughtful questions and listening carefully to the responses. Depending on the project, you might ask one or several of these questions:

- What kind of pushback do you think we might get on this idea from those directly affected?

- What will be key steps in your process to roll out this project next quarter?

- What's a realistic date to complete a project like this?

- What suppliers do you think we should involve?

- Do you anticipate any delays along the way as we work on this initiative?

- The budget I've set aside is $X. Does that amount seem sufficient?

- What concerns do you have at this point?

As staff members respond to your questions, you can verify for *yourself* their understanding of your goals and their expected deliverables—while there's still time to make a course correction or amplify.

> Effective communicators know that their **body language** and **behavior trump** their words.

Leaving this strategic alignment of goals and expectations to chance can sink your ship before it leaves the harbor.

CHAPTER 4

Build a Culture of Trust

If my people understand me, I'll get their attention.
If my people trust me, I'll get their action.

—CAVETT ROBERT, MOTIVATIONAL SPEAKER

If you've ever worked with liars, you understand how quickly their deception can destroy relationships, dampen morale, and poison the culture of an organization. One such incident comes quickly to mind.

Devin (his name changed to protect the guilty) announced that the roof of the building had been damaged during a windstorm. As operations manager, he needed to have it repaired. But preoccupied with other things and seeing no immediate problem with leaks, he postposed filing an insurance claim or calling a repair company to investigate the situation. Weeks turned into months.

When the next windstorm hit, Devin's CEO asked him about the previous repairs. Caught off guard, Devin responded in his typical manner—with a lie: "Oh, that. Yeah, sure. The crew has already been out here and repaired most of it. I scheduled it back during the holidays when most employees were off—for minimal disruption. Just took them a few days to get it done."

"Good."

"They just need one more day for replacing a few gutters to have it all finished. I'm going to try to schedule them out here again in the next week or two to get those last gutters up."

"Great." His boss walked away, satisfied that all was well with the roof.

Later that day, through another series of events, the boss discovered that Devin had scheduled no roof repairs at all. When he confronted Devin with the truth, Devin admitted that he'd simply forgotten about the roof damage. He explained his plan to take care of the repairs the following weekend.

To Devin, no harm done. Repairs made. No rain in the forecast. No problem.

To his boss, big harm done. Trust lost.

Strong communicators trade on trust. It's their currency. When trust has been developed and tested over time, the relationship remains rock-solid. When your coworkers, customers, and family trust you, they listen to your input, support your work, and remain loyal in difficult times.

Without trust, a relationship goes bankrupt. The distrusted communicator's words carry no more weight than currency from an overthrown government or stock from a bankrupt corporation.

So how do you build a culture of trust in your organization and in your own relationships?

Strong **communicators** trade on **TRUST**. It's their **currency**.

BUILDING TRUST IN YOUR
ORGANIZATION AND RELATIONSHIPS

- Tell the truth. Avoid deception in all its forms.

- Give your reasons for the actions you take and the decisions you make. Be transparent.

- Make your actions match your words. Be sure what you say in public matches what you do in private.

- Demonstrate competence. No matter how much we like somebody, we trust those people who have a track record of performance—whether it's developing software, designing business processes, or driving forklifts.

- Show humility. Be approachable, not arrogant and aloof. Be friendly and likeable, not a know-it-all who must have the last word on every topic in every discussion.

- Demonstrate confidence. If you don't believe in yourself, why should others?

- Have a positive outlook. For the most part, people want to trust those who are upbeat rather than negative. People need hope in the future.

- Trust others. If you distrust others, most often they return the "favor."

Without a foundation of trust, you have no platform for authentic communication.

CHAPTER 5

Hire Based on Core Character and Competency

*When hiring key employees, there are only
two qualities to look for: judgment and taste.
Almost everything else can be bought by the yard.*

—JOHN W. GARDNER,
FORMER US SECRETARY OF HEALTH, EDUCATION,
AND WELFARE IN THE LYNDON JOHNSON ADMINISTRATION

Shelves are full of books that tell you how to hire well. But because this book addresses communication, I'll focus in this chapter on the key event: the interview. Your success often depends on the emotional intelligence of those you hire in strategic positions. That means you need to make hiring decisions based on information other than gut instincts and first impressions.

You'll want to discover the *complete* package you're getting: personality traits, self-awareness, true attitudes and values, emotional stability, motivations and intentions, and interpersonal skills. Psychologists insist that asking candidates about how they've handled past situations provides far more valuable insights than asking them about hypothetical situations:

Not: "What would you do if a customer did X?"

But: "Tell me about a stressful customer interaction and how you handled it."

Not: "How do you feel about cold-calling inactive clients."

But: "Can you tell me about three inactive clients in your last job that you discovered in your organization's database and what steps you took to turn them into active customers again?"

Interviews require well-planned questions that solicit answers that reflect genuine attributes, opinions, and skills. Many applicants have rehearsed for likely questions, so ask for two or three examples to get past the practiced answers and gain real insights.

Consider the following interview questions to produce meaningful information about the core character and competence of your potential job candidates:

Who has been a favorite coworker, client, supplier, or boss of yours in the past? Why do you think the two of you worked well together?
Have your candidate identify the person first before you ask the follow-up question. Be sure not to jump to conclusions about *why* the two worked well together. Their simpatico relationship may have been a result of similar personalities—or complementary traits. For example, your applicant might be a disorganized person who worked well with someone extremely attentive to detail, following behind to correct mistakes or oversights!

***W**hat irritates you most about
other people you've worked with?*

Smart candidates will probably tell you that they get along with everyone. But probe more deeply for their true feelings about having to accommodate other people: Can you tell me about one of these "less than favorite people" at another job? What specific things did that person do that seemed to annoy other coworkers? Why was that *not* annoying to you? If it *was* annoying to you, how did you manage to cope with those habits or attitudes? With this question, you gain insight into applicants' flexibility and their capability for empathy, along with their values.

***T**ell me about three people in the public eye
or your personal life whom you admire and why.*

Responses here will reveal several things: How informed are they on current affairs, politics, or pop culture? Does their response suggest they can't think of anyone, or simply that they can't narrow their choices? Were all choices from public life rather than personal acquaintances? That response may suggest they have few mentors or role models. Why? If all choices are personal acquaintances, that answer may suggest noninvolvement in the community. Why? At least answers will reveal candidates' values.

***W**hat are the biggest ways people waste time on the job?
What do you think are the reasons for this?*

Time wasters on the job are routinely discussed and reported: chatting with coworkers, surfing the web, gaming, personal shopping, and personal phone calls. What you're looking for is defensiveness, discomfort, or dishonesty in your applicants' answers. Or do they analyze "time wasters" and productivity at a higher level, seeing sources of the problem? For example, do they cite improper workflow, lack of training, indecisiveness, nonfunctional teams and conflict, or insufficient equipment? The level of their analysis clues you in to the level of their thinking in general.

*H*ave you ever seen anyone
mistreated in the workplace?
How did you handle the situation?

Their answers will reveal values and ethics. You're also judging their capacity to feel empathy and compassion. Further, the action they took in this situation suggests their ability to persuade others and their tolerance for risk (if they had to act alone to stop the mistreatment). Did they risk their own reputation or even their job to do the right thing?

*D*o you remember Judith Viorst's children's book
Alexander and the Terrible, Horrible, No Good, Very Bad Day?
*Tell me about a horrible day you've had this past year
and how you dealt with it.*

Their response gives you some perspective on what happenings they consider "routine" versus "horrible." But what you're really looking for is their coping mechanisms—both emotional stability and resourcefulness. Listen carefully to the retelling for phrases such as "so upset," "so angry," "had a major meltdown," "went ballistic," "frantic," and "just beside myself with worry." Did they finally solve the problems, or did someone else have to take charge? How much and for how long did this trouble affect their work and their life? How does their idea of "serious" compare with yours? Does their reaction seem appropriate or extreme?

*W*hat has been your biggest accomplishment to date?
The second biggest? The third biggest?
Why are these three things important to you?

Again, their answers reveal character traits and values. Are they sharing all work-related accomplishments? Personal or family accomplishments? How do they rank the three things named? Reasons reveal much about applicants' view of success, meaningful work, and the importance of others in their lives.

*T*ell me about a time that you failed.
What did you learn from the experience?

If they have never failed, either they are lying or they are extremely risk-averse. Do they blame others or accept responsibility for the failure? Do they seem teachable? What does their attitude say about humility or arrogance?

*E*xplain a new idea to me. For example, take a complex process,
product, or service in your current job and explain it to me so
well that I could teach a class on it tomorrow.

I've yet to meet the job applicant who admits to lacking communication skills. In my three decades of reviewing résumés and hiring, job candidates always claim to have some version of "excellent communication skills," "good oral and written communication skills," or "great people skills." This question aims to test those skills. As the applicant replies, pose questions at various stages to see how they react.

Do they overview the idea clearly and then fill in details? Do they organize their thoughts logically? Do they skip steps and definitions, assuming you know more than you do? Does their body language convey impatience with questions? Do they show arrogance, by talking down to you? Their communication during this "explanation" will likely be similar to that used with coworkers or customers.

> Reasons reveal much about
> applicants' **view of success**, **meaningful** work,
> and the **importance** of others in their lives.

Of course, your questions must meet the job criteria. But these questions assume that the job you're hiring for demands good communication skills and good judgment. Given that's a valid assumption, these nine questions can mean the difference between a strategic hire and a costly termination.

CHAPTER 6

Nix Micromanaging and Other Negatives

To persuade is more trouble than to dominate, and
the powerful seldom take this trouble if they can avoid it.

—CHARLES HORTON COOLEY,
SOCIOLOGIST AND AUTHOR

I f leaders' liabilities (negatives) overpower their assets, their team members begin to tune them out—emotionally, if not literally. Yes, they have to respond to texts, emails, or phone calls to keep their jobs. But engagement evaporates.

If you haven't worked for one of these micromanaging, overbearing bosses, you've heard about them. Employees buzz about such bosses over lunch, complain about them around the water cooler, and chew them up at the dinner table with their family. At the least, for the individual reporting to this kind of manager, frustration leads to deep-seated resentment that often triggers a job change or career move. (A Gallup study of 7,272 US adults found that one in two left their job to get away from their manager.[3])

You, as a leader, want to avoid these negatives to prevent a wall of resentment from building and blocking your communication with staff and peers.

LIABILITY #1: EXPOSING THE HOLE IN THE DONUT— THE MISTAKE, THE MISSTEP, THE MISUNDERSTANDING

Some managers never seem to focus on the perfect circle. Instead, their first comment calls attention to the inconsequential mistake. They ask for trivial backup data that you failed to bring with you to the presentation. They imply that maybe you have misunderstood the politics surrounding the situation and therefore have written the email with a more aggressive tone than appropriate. In a meeting, rather than focusing on the positive result of your project, they zoom in on your mistake: the "gotcha."

These micromanagers may

- Distrust you for any number of reasons
- Fear you and fear losing control if they don't keep close watch on you
- Attempt to boost their self-esteem by lowering yours with tight controls, with threats that instill fear of firing, and with constant put-downs and corrections

They feel frightened, out of control, and frustrated at the increased workload their micromanaging causes.

So if you work for a micromanaging boss, your first two challenges: Develop trust. Help your boss feel secure. Tall order.

If you suspect that *you* are the micromanager, same answer: Develop trust so you can feel secure yourself. Distrust comes from faulty assumptions about other people's intentions.

Antidote: Practice direct communication. Ask questions. Listen carefully to the answers before you draw conclusions. State directly what you expect, need, or want.

> Some managers never seem to focus on the **perfect circle**. Instead, their first comment calls attention to the **inconsequential mistake**.

LIABILITY #2: MICROMANAGING THE PROCESS RATHER THAN STATING THE GOAL

Effective leaders assign a project, state the goal, provide the resources, communicate any warnings or safeguards, and state any required check-back points along the way. Then they let you go about your task until it's completed. Less effective managers, however, haven't learned how to delegate. Instead, they assign a project, blindfold team members as to where they're going, and then lead them through the process. Result: A huge waste of time for the manager and frustration for the team.

Antidote: Learn to delegate the goal to a qualified person, provide resources, clarify at what points you'd like him or her to check back with you, and leave the specific process to that person. (For more elaboration on the six steps in delegating effectively, see my earlier book *Communicate With Confidence*.)

LIABILITY #3: IMPERSONATING A KNOW-IT-ALL

Although great leaders learn to hire people smarter than they are in key disciplines, less confident managers feel out of control around brilliant staff members and colleagues. So they have to keep reminding others that they are the smartest person in the room. They communicate that know-it-all attitude in various ways: by doing all the talking, by refusing to listen to new ideas, by lots of I-told-you-so lines and a plethora of war stories.

Antidote: Force yourself to listen at least 10 minutes or to at least three people—whichever comes first—before you speak up in a meeting.

LIABILITY #4: PLAYING HIDE-AND-SEEK

The disappearing boss is here today and gone tomorrow. In the office at 10:00. Missing in action at 2:00. Mysteriously back to work at 4:00. Comes in at 11:00 the following day. Ask why, and the explanation makes perfect sense to that person: "I don't owe you an explanation. I can work from anywhere. I've put in 50 hours already this week."

What this disappearing boss doesn't understand is why someone needs to know his or her physical location: to sign documents, to attend an on-site meeting, to meet with a VIP customer, to answer an unexpected question, to make a quick emergency decision. If not in the office, can the boss be interrupted? If so, during what hours? If the CEO or a VIP client calls, when will the boss be able to return the call or answer the email? What should the staff promise callers and visitors? All are legitimate questions.

Being unable to get in touch with a disappearing boss creates frustration—not to mention leaving a bad impression with clients and colleagues. But to the disappearing boss, it's all about power and control.

Antidote: Leave information with someone or in an accessible place about how you can be reached in an emergency. Then define an "emergency," and state when you will again be available.

LIABILITY #5: ANNOUNCING OR CANCELING STAFF MEETINGS AT THE LAST MINUTE

Either action implies that no one's schedule counts but the manager's. Everyone else's productivity plummets as they reshuffle the day's projects—including client commitments. Last-minute or overtime meetings send a strong message to outsiders waiting for attention: "The manager here has decided your customers or colleagues don't matter. Tough luck."

Antidote: As part of your team's ground rules for meetings, agree on what constitutes the basis for an emergency meeting: Input when you're about to lose a big client? Major headquarters announcement? Staff shortages due to an epidemic and the need to reschedule workflow for the day? For all other reasons, agree that meetings will be scheduled with XX hours' lead time.

Leading and communicating with a team of diverse personalities can be a challenging proposition. Why increase the odds for dissension with any of these liabilities that cause people to disengage over work *habits* that have nothing to do with their actual work?

Strategic decisions about managing time and people quickly become daily routines that communicate far more than words.

CHAPTER 7

Squelch the Urge to Hoard

The art of communication is the language of leadership.

—JAMES HUMES, FORMER SPEECHWRITER
FOR FIVE US PRESIDENTS

Many children grow up singing this song in church:

This little light of mine,
I'm gonna let it shine.
This little light of mine,
I'm gonna let it shine.
This little light of mine,
I'm gonna let it shine.
Let it shine, let it shine, let it shine!

Hide it under a bushel? No!
I'm gonna let it shine.
Hide it under a bushel? No!
I'm gonna let it shine.
Hide it under a bushel? No!
I'm gonna let it shine.
Let it shine, let it shine, let it shine!

But somewhere between elementary age and the workplace, some people do decide to hide their light—their creativity, insights, passion—along with information, decisions, and reasoning that would help others do their own job better. Instead, they adopt an "every person or department for himself/herself" attitude.

Jack, a coaching client of mine and the vice president of a large auto manufacturer, seemed bewildered by the fact that his boss had suggested that he contact me for communication coaching as part of his career development plan. As Jack explained to me—several times—during our session, "I run the largest division in the company. We're responsible for more than 15 percent of the company's revenue—and a much larger share of profit than any other division."

But according to Jack's boss, CEO of the parent company, Jack's performance in his functional role was not the problem. On the contrary. His CEO summed things up this way: "Jack's a lone ranger. He sits in our executive meetings totally tuned out. He acts bored, aloof, arrogant. Never comments on issues his peers raise about plans or challenges they're facing in their own divisions. Runs a good organization. But seems totally unwilling to share his expertise with his peers. He doesn't seem to understand that part of what we pay him for is his thought leadership—his willingness to contribute ideas to the entire organization. See if you can't get that point across to him."

I did. As we talked, the notion that his organization paid him not only to run his division but also to share his expertise and information with peers seemed foreign to him. When I stated the idea to him directly, he looked as though I'd hit him across the face with a two-by-four. He sat stunned. Finally, he said, "Hmmm. Really? They expect me to help the other guys? Give them ideas about what I do in my division? Hmmm." He nodded, looking as if the concept of sharing information and "thought leadership" had never occurred to him.

And that was that. End of discussion.

You have probably heard this common communication complaint: "Everyone's working in silos. Nobody knows what's going on." People hoard information for many reasons—from innocent to sinister. They

- Think they have limited or no time to share information
- Can't decide what to pass on—what's significant and what's trivial
- Don't know what or why others need to know

- Withhold information to punish others

- Withhold information to feel smarter than others

- Withhold information to feel "on the inside" with special information

- Withhold information to cause others to make mistakes and appear dumb

- Withhold information to control a situation

- Withhold information because when they share it and get no response, they think nobody cares

All understandable reasons—just not *good* ones.

By definition, real leaders share strategic information. Because they focus on big-picture performance, problems, issues, and results, they understand that significant information doesn't "belong" to them. Just as scientists who finish a major study rush to publish their test results so that other researchers can build on their work, business leaders share their metrics, ideas, and solutions inside their organization so that other internal leaders can improve their own performance and build on these successes.

The more helpful information they share, the faster these leaders are considered "clearinghouses" for the latest thinking and buzz inside their organization—and often their reputation spreads outside the organization as well.

Understand your strategic role as a content curator.

CHAPTER 8

Guide With Strategic Questions

The manager asks how and when;
the leader asks what and why.

—WARREN BENNIS, AUTHOR, PROFESSOR,
AND CONSULTANT FOCUSING ON LEADERSHIP

S trategic thinkers use leading questions to advance a discussion and their case.

For example, maybe your organization exhibits at an industry trade show every year. In the weekly staff meeting, the agenda item surfaces and your team begins to discuss new ways to generate traffic to your booth. You might raise the provocative question, "Could we generate *more positive* industry buzz by *not* attending the trade show this year? I'm thinking of three organizations which did exactly that in their respective industries recently." Give your examples, and then wait for others to ponder the question.

A second example: A colleague proposes a 20 percent price hike for one of your product lines. You oppose the idea. But instead of making a statement, you guide the discussion that follows with these questions: "How did you arrive at the 20 percent increase rather than 18 or 22?"

"If the goal is to increase profits overall, why this product to make the first step up?" "Is there another product line that might be more suitable for a test price hike?" "What's the fallback position if our market share drops?"

With such a series of questions, you can lead an individual or a group to rethink positions or decisions without setting a direct challenge and without stating your position. The beauty of this approach? Once they voice answers to your questions, people "buy" their own data and reasoning:

Do take care in how you structure your questions:

Start with open-ended questions. "In what way do you mean?" "Will you describe that situation in more detail?" "How so?" "What would you say is the best way to go about doing that?" "What's your reaction so far to the plans you've heard from Gloria?"

Listen to their answers and then ask follow-up questions. Don't stop with just one or two follow-up questions. Probe several layers: "Why is that?" "When does that happen?" "How much do you estimate that might cost?" "Are there any exceptions to that?"

Ask them to separate fact from opinion. Often it's difficult to tell which is which. You might have to ask, "Specifically what experience or incident are you referring to?" "Would all experts agree with the conclusions you've stated?" "What are some of the differing opinions from other experts on this?" "What's your source on that?" "Do you *know* that's a fact, or do you *think* that's a fact?" "Can you please forward to me those statistics (or that study, that article, that link)?"

Ask for collaboration or disagreement. "Who else do you think agrees with you on that?" "Have you thought about who might disagree with you on that?"

Provide plenty of silence. As the father of modern management, Peter Drucker advised us to listen for what's not said. You'll hear a lot that may surprise you. (Silence can be particularly powerful in interviewing job applicants.)

For an expanded discussion of all these techniques and many more (45 listening tips in total), plus a plethora of examples, see my earlier book *Communicate With Confidence*.

A statement of opinion sets up either agreement or disagreement—often rock-solid disagreement, even hostility. A well-phrased question, by contrast, generates thought and opens up new possibilities.

> ## Strategic thinkers
> use leading questions
> to advance
> a **discussion** and
> **their cause**.

CHAPTER 9

Dislodge Log-Jamming Directives

*To get what you want, you must communicate
to others in a way that inspires them to give it to you.*

—MARSHALL SYLVER, SPEAKER
AND ENTERTAINER

Leaders especially want to make their mark on operations, stamp their philosophical footprint on minds, and leave their legacy on hearts and in hallways. They hope their work will be unique, pleasant, and profitable. Understandable goals. No leader intentionally creates a logjam. They want to set clear goals and increase productivity. No one intentionally delays or stops work that needs to be done.

All too often, however, *new* leaders (or seasoned leaders taking over in a new position) start out with directives or statements that set their team up for disappointment rather than the intended positive reaction and productivity boost. No matter the *intention*, the result is often delay, disillusionment, disengagement, and even derision.

"Give me your wish list, as if money were no object." Generally tossed out during strategic planning meetings or retreats, this comment—meant to start a brainstorming exercise—sounds like a generous gesture. The leader wants input on needs: What resources do staff members need to get the job done faster or better? Equipment? Tools? More people? Space?

The problem with this goodwill gesture from the new leader? Money is *always* an object—even when you have plenty of it. Even if venture capitalists have just dropped $200 million in your pocket, you'll have to justify why one project gets funded and another doesn't. When new manager after new manager arrives and encourages people to "dream big," but there's no basis for thinking the fairy godmother will fund the dream, this approach becomes tiresome to the troops. It simply takes everyone's time to submit ideas and saps their emotional energy to see no result from the effort.

"I'd like us to blow this up and try to rebuild it from the ground up." For all our complaining, most of us are attached to our work. We take pride in our achievements. Yes, we're open to progress, change, improvements, growth. But to have a new leader walk in and talk about "rebuilding" implies that what has gone before has become worthless. Many employees consider it arrogance for a new leader to begin "change for change's sake" before he or she knows what's what and why what's what.

Whether you're talking about processes, procedures, or products, understand that phrasing counts. "Modify," maybe. "Upgrade," probably. But "rebuild" will most often create a wall of resistance.

"Let's put everything on hold until I get a better understanding." What does "on hold" mean? Literally stop work? Stop planning? Stop doing? Stop funding? Stop signing contracts? Notify all departments/people related to the project? For how long? Do what in the meantime? What if "this" is my primary job at the moment? This comment sets up a major logjam, with the boss blocking workflow.

A more positive phrasing: "I'm going to put my plans on hold for a few weeks until I do some listening. I want to hear about your projects and progress, get your opinions on what you're doing and why, and gather your feedback. Then we can move forward together."

"Check back with me before we make a final commitment on that." This directive has the same effect as the previous one—a bottleneck while productivity decreases to a spurt here and there. The only difference with this comment is the additional fear it generates with the "until I get a better understanding" omitted. Employees may fear this check-back directive suggests the leader's ongoing management style: tight control with little room for personal initiative and decision making.

A more positive phrasing: "Please keep me updated as things move along until I can get myself up to speed on your projects."

If you're a new leader, winning the trust of your team will be one of your top priorities. To do that, instead of immediately issuing directives, listen. Take a breath to find out what's in play and how the score stands. Ask about individual goals. Share your goals with the team. And then invite them to join your mission. From the very beginning, they need to see you as a real partner—not a roadblock to their productivity.

CHAPTER 10

Become a Coach, Not a Critic

*Praise works with only three types
of people: men, women, and children.*

—UNKNOWN

Y ou're not *really* going to eat a second serving, are you?" "Is that on your diet?" "You've sure put on a few pounds over the summer, haven't you?" Ask anyone who has ever tried to lose weight about their reaction to a spouse or parent who continually nags with comments like these.

Then ask that same person to compare results in losing weight while working with an encouraging coach (or even an online program with canned feedback): "Good work!" "Impressive!" "You've gained two pounds. But don't give up. Just get back on your personal eating plan. You can do this!"

I repeat: Ask any dieter which approach works best, coaching or critiquing, and I guarantee they'll select the coach every time. Ditto for the workplace.

Life coaches and personal trainers seem to be the new status symbols. From corporate CEOs to the seventeen-year-old language student, everyone's talking about their personal fitness trainer or their financial accountability coach. Like bosses, coaches expect you to show up, work hard, and do what you say you will. Accountability, encouragement, and support prove to be far greater motivators than judgment and criticism.

Here's how you as a team leader or manager can become a strategic coach rather than simply a critic.

Help your team members identify their strengths. As far as you have the power to do so, put people in positions and on projects that allow them to use those strengths to shine. Far too many people struggle, working in jobs (sometimes lifelong careers) that do not make use of their strengths. No matter how much training and mentoring they receive, at best, they'll improve those "weaknesses" until they become only "average" performers.[4]

> Ask any dieter which approach works best,
> **coaching or critiquing**, and I guarantee
> they'll select the coach every time.
>
> Ditto for the workplace.

Communicate the goal, any specific expectations, and clear standards to measure success. Make sure team members know the desired outcome. Specify any processes they have to follow to achieve the goal (legal, organizational, industry-specific). How will they know they've been successful? What are the specific measurements? Due dates? Quality ratings? Complaints handled per hour? Widgets completed? Absence of mistakes? Money saved?

Provide resources. What's the budget? Overtime hours? Extra head count? Access to equipment, training, experts, or data?

Build confidence. Your belief in them inspires their own confidence. Their commitment to you—and possibly to other team members—in writing that they will accomplish X by Y date and having you believe in them starts the adrenaline pumping.

Warn of potential danger ahead. Coaches help develop safeguards so that weaknesses won't waylay a person's overall success. In other words, as a coach you'll help ward off problems before they develop. With projects or plans that may be in jeopardy, point out trouble spots and suggest check-back points for further direction before problems reach a crisis.

Give clear feedback. In the study conducted by the authors of *The 2020 Workplace* and discussed in their book by the same title, Jeanne Meister and Karie Willyerd point out that the ability employees most want in their leaders ("straight feedback") is what's most lacking. As judged by HR professionals, leaders lack both the will and the skill to provide helpful feedback to their team members.

To address the "will" part of the equation, understand that your team wants and needs to hear from you about their performance—even if your feedback is less than glowing. When you first begin to work together, let them know that feedback is "what we do in this department" and that they'll be receiving feedback and coaching often as "an investment in their career growth." Mention that philosophy as your modus operandi for accomplishing great things.

To address the "skill" part of any reluctance to give candid feedback, start with questions. Ask how the people involved think the X or Y project is going. Listen and evaluate their perspective. State your own observations, describing rather than labeling. Here's an example: "During the three hours I was in the trade-show booth, I noticed that we had heavy traffic. But at least fifty percent of the traffic was not our ideal customer. The pre-show marketing piece missed the target. It drew the mid-manager rather than the executive buyer."

Clear feedback can be the difference between success and failure, between attracting great talent and mediocre players, between retaining the best and watching them leave to learn elsewhere.

Offer encouragement. Be liberal with supportive comments when you see staff or colleagues doing well, even after small steps along the way. If you're a runner—particularly, a marathoner—you know that supporters along the route cheering you on make a big difference. If you've ever tried to lose weight, hearing "you're looking good" every five pounds or so certainly reinforces your commitment to healthy eating.

Provide stretch assignments to help others gain experience and deepen expertise. For example, is there a feasibility study that might gain traction with the executive team and also provide opportunity for them to interview key executives about their three-year goals for the organization? Could you suggest that they participate on a company-wide project team that will stretch their thinking?

Celebrate wins. A coach's slap on the back and "Great game" after a win feels much better than his or her walking away with a muttered "Done" or, worse, with head down and mumbling, "You've got work to do for the next game."

Whether you communicate as a coach or critic always comes down to a strategic decision—one that affects productivity, morale, absenteeism, and turnover—and ultimately shapes your culture for years. To sum up: Lead the ride from the side. Critique food, wine, and movies; coach people.

CHAPTER 11

Give Kudos That Count

*A good leader takes a little more than his share
of the blame, a little less than his share of the credit.*

—ARNOLD H. GLASOW,
BUSINESSMAN AND HUMORIST

Have you ever tried to *act* surprised for a "surprise" birthday party? Difficult, right? Pretending to be thrilled about a recognition that routinely comes your way every month is equally difficult. Nor does that recognition continue to motivate. In fact, you may notice the recognition only when it stops coming and starts demotivating.

Let me explain: Recognizing employees for work well done improves overall performance, but not in the way you might think. Those winning the kudos don't necessarily work harder—but those *not recognized* do.

That conclusion follows from a study reported in a paper released from CESifo, a European research center, and authored by Dr. Robert Dru, professor of economics at Erasmus University Rotterdam in the Netherlands.[5] The experiment involved assigning groups of students to three hours of data entry. Some high-performing individuals received

GUIDELINES FOR EMPLOYEE RECOGNITION

- Personalize recognition. Individuals, not groups, do work.

- Make recognition motivating, not embarrassing, for star performers. Make those recognized part of an elite *group*— don't focus on the solo star. Singling them out may create envy and isolate them from their peers.[6]

- Keep recognition a surprise, not routine. When employees become conditioned to expect rewards, they feel disappointed when they aren't acknowledged—but not necessarily pleased when they do receive praise. The expected reward no longer motivates.

- Make it clear why the person deserves recognition. Praise the specific performance, skill, judgment, expertise, or accomplishment.

- Share stories with your group to help them understand the impact of their work on both internal and external customers. Show them that their work makes a difference! Important work that serves humanity or saves lives, of course, brings great personal satisfaction. But even increasing revenues, cutting costs, and improving profits matter, too—if workers feel that they contributed significantly to others.

- Make the recognition personal and heartfelt. People get "likes" and "comments" all day on their YouTube videos, Facebook posts, LinkedIn shares, and Pinterest pins. Your recognition has to up the ante.

- Vary the reward: recognition from a top executive, attention from you as their immediate supervisor, time off, gift certificates or a prize, trips, training, introductions to senior leaders, more responsibility, acknowledgment in front of peers, or money. You've heard the cliché "Money talks." Today, many workers will trade a salary increase or a bonus for time off. Don't assume that you know which recognition speaks louder or motivates longer.

Ensure that your recognition accomplishes its purpose.

a thank-you note for their "hard work" during their shift. Those notes increased the productivity of those groups for the rest of their shift—most notably for the workers who had performed the worst before the thank-you notes arrived. Students *not* recognized by a special note learned that their productivity was low, compared to colleagues. That led to embarrassment.

Another conclusion from the study: The overall performance increase was greatest when several workers were recognized—not just one of the group and not the entire group. From this and other studies on recognition, leaders can learn to give kudos strategically to motivate *all* employees—the weaker performers as well as the star performers.

Kudos to you as a leader for identifying how best to use recognition as a strategic motivator to increase overall job satisfaction and individual productivity.

CHAPTER 12

Fire People to Be Fair

*I never make the mistake of arguing with
people for whose opinions I have no respect.*

—EDWARD GIBBON, 18TH-CENTURY
ENGLISH AUTHOR AND HISTORIAN

How long before you know if a new hire is going to work out in a job?"
I often pose that question to executives at client organizations.

Their answers vary from "a few weeks" to "three to six months."
But the most troubling situation seems to be correcting those mis-hire
decisions quickly. Although most leaders embrace the adage "Hire
slowly, fire fast," they dread those dismissal conversations and struggle
far too long, trying to correct a bad hiring decision.

But to be fair to all concerned—the organization, other team members, and the person being fired—leaders need to change the way they
think about terminating someone's employment. A termination is a
logical result of an employee's job performance. Their employee's
work, behavior, attitude, or skill (or lack thereof) has led to the outcome. The decision to terminate is simply the final step in the process.

CONSIDER EVERYONE'S STRESS

The firing doesn't seem so difficult when someone has flagrantly violated company policy. Such conversations prove far more difficult when the person's expertise simply does not make the grade—that is, when the job has outgrown the employee's skill set. But in both cases, you want to be fair to *all* the players involved in the work situation.

Team members know when a coworker isn't pulling his or her weight. Yes, they may "cover" for a weak performer. They may remain silent and "grin and bear it." But their own workload increases as they watch and wait to see how the leader handles the problem.

Your organization must absorb the cost of a poor player—nonproductivity, mistakes, rework, morale. You yourself have to spend extra time in supervising, in coaching, and maybe in disciplinary actions.

Finally, underperformers themselves feel stress when they don't meet job standards. It's not fair to keep an employee in a job with false expectations that the situation will improve or that standards will be lowered to his or her performance level. The person feels tense just waiting for the ax to fall.

DOCUMENT YOUR DISCUSSIONS AS PREP

Theo called the head of HR into his office: "Just want to get your approval on this before I take action. I need to let Kimberly go."

"Why?"

"She's just not working out."

"But why specifically?"

"She's just not working out. Several things."

"Have you had discussions with her? Given her a chance to correct those things? Documented those discussions?"

Theo shook his head no to all these basic actions.

This scenario happens so often it is a classic case study in an HR manual. Don't repeat the mistake. You need to provide feedback, tell the employee specifically what changes he needs to make, and give him opportunity to improve the performance. Then document your conversation, summarizing the issues under discussion and capturing the employee's response. If you've given the employee an improvement plan, include those details in your note, date it, and file it. If the employee doesn't make changes in a reasonable amount of time, then you move to the next step—either a second warning or termination. (This file documentation provides support should difficulty develop later in the process.)

COMMUNICATE YOUR DECISION TO THE EMPLOYEE

If you're a compassionate person, telling someone they're fired will never be easy. In three decades as CEO of my own small company, I've had to fire very few people (one for stealing equipment, two for excessive absences, two for repeatedly lying about projects/assignments, and only five for underperformance). Even firing the one for stealing proved a difficult situation because she was a competent employee and very likable.

So don't wait until you're "up for it" to make the decision. You will *never* be up for it unless you have a heart of stone. But think strategically.

Adopt the appropriate mindset. Acknowledge that dismissing someone will be hard. Understand that leaders must make tough decisions. Know that after the emotions of the immediate situation fade, the underperformer will feel relieved of the stress of failure. He or she will be able to move into a more successful position somewhere else.

Prepare for the conversation. Decide when and where you will have the conversation. Plan the phrasing. How will you summarize the reason? What's the effective date of the dismissal? Immediate? At the end of the day? Does your organization give outplacement support? What's the policy about comments to a future employer—to verify only dates of employment and positions held? Be ready to explain how and when the rest of the team will be told about the termination.

Avoid arguing. This is not the time to rehash the employee's performance or listen to an appeal. Simply restate your decision. "We've made the decision to let you go." Restate it after an appeal: "I'm sorry, Bill, but we're going to have to end your employment." Restate it again if necessary: "I hear you, Bill. But the decision has already been made. Our outplacement service can be very helpful to you. I hope you'll take advantage of that."

Do not focus on yourself. Comments like "This is the part of my job that I dislike the most" or "I hate this as much as you do" will only anger the other person. Although such comments may make you feel less guilty, they are simply meant to win sympathy for yourself—definitely inappropriate in conversations of this nature.

Demonstrate compassion and sensitivity. Prepare for the employee's emotions—everything from anger to devastation. Examine your planned phrasing for "hot words." Eliminate comments that sound pompous, parental, or heartless: "You've been unwilling to. . ." "You've ignored all my attempts to help you." "I've given you far more than your fair share of time and attention to improve, but you haven't taken any responsibility for yourself. You leave me no choice but to. . ."

Never treat employees as if they are criminals—unless they are, of course. In that case, you'll need to press charges or risk having your firing decision judged as unfair or illegal. Otherwise, let them leave their dignity intact. Remember the Golden Rule and handle the conversation accordingly.

Effective leaders never like to fire employees. In fact, they loathe the task. But that action represents a strategic decision leaders need to communicate for the well-being of the entire team—its morale and future growth.

CHAPTER 13

Energize Rather Than Demoralize

You must become what you want to attract.

—MARSHALL SYLVER,
SPEAKER AND ENTERTAINER

The caller early Monday morning identified herself as the CEO of a large commercial real estate firm. I listened as she introduced herself again, reminding me that we'd met a year earlier when she had accompanied her daughter to our training center to be groomed for her rise to executive management in the family business.

"I need to meet with you *today*," the caller said. "Preferably in the next hour or two. Can you come here? That would be better. Or I can come there if I have to. . . . My head is splitting. You're out by the airport, if I recall? Off 121?"

"That's correct. . . . What can I help you with? Can you tell me a little more about what the issue is?"

"My life's falling apart. Everybody here is driving me crazy. I don't know—maybe it's me. I've just got to talk to somebody. Now. This morning."

My caller's voice broke. She sounded like an exhausted young mom with triplets who'd just kept her up all night with a bad virus—not like the seasoned sixty-something executive I remembered from a year earlier.

"Okay. Can you give me some details? Is it a communication issue specifically or a more general management concern?"

"Everybody who comes through the door has a problem. . . . Like some deal has gone south, and they want help. Or they don't like some policy. They're up in arms about *something*. Nobody's happy! Infighting! *Nobody* gets along! My daughter—they hate her. Or at least they won't listen to her. They all still come to me for everything. I can't get away for one minute. Nobody cooperates on anything! . . . I've got to talk to an outsider to get some perspective on all this."

Mind you, I'm not a life coach or a psychologist. Typical calls to our office come from *calm* professionals wanting to book a speech or asking for coaching on executive presence, presentation skills, or another communication challenge. This CEO sounded as though her emotional pendulum were swinging between management mayhem and murder.

"Are you talking about at work or your family?" I probed.

"Both."

The entire scene from a year earlier was coming back to me as I listened to Eleanor. She had scheduled the appointment for her daughter to work with me for half a day to increase her executive presence. The daughter had just finished graduate school and returned home to join the business.

Before I could respond to Eleanor, she continued, "So maybe it's just all *me*. Maybe it's *my* management style. Maybe *I'm* the one who's causing the problem—keeping everything all stirred up. I just need to talk to somebody NOW. So do you do that kind of coaching?"

"Well, if it's a communication problem with your staff, I can help you with *that*, certainly. But I'm not a psychologist. You sound very upset. I'm willing to rearrange my work schedule and come out to meet with you today."

"Then send me a proposal . . . and I'll get back to you—either later today or tomorrow. Or next week."

At that point, I *did* identify the management problem at her organization!

I've never met a manager who intended to demoralize their staff or project team. Many do, but that's not their *intention*. As I talk with them or those who report to them, what surfaces are attitudes, practices, and skill deficiencies that lead their employees to disrespect, disengage, and decide to leave for a more pleasant environment.

When an executive at the top of the organization notices that a manager is struggling to keep good people and suggests that that manager come for communication coaching, it doesn't take long in our interviewing process before we observe troubling communication habits.

Personal stories (often from the perplexed managers themselves trying to pinpoint the reason for their ineffectiveness) present striking differences in two categories of people—those who motivate versus those who demoralize.

DEMORALIZING MANAGERS VERSUS MOTIVATING MANAGERS

Demoralizing Managers	Motivating Managers
Dole out information in bits and pieces—as if they are a parent, parceling out only what they think their "children" are able to handle at the moment.	Communicate the big picture.
Focus on the *how*. They fear that if they offer the *why*, people may ask questions or challenge decisions.	Explain the *why* behind decisions, projects, and tasks.
Discourage questions and see them as time wasters and challenges to authority.	Welcome questions as an avenue to collaboration, engagement, and innovation.

DEMORALIZING MANAGERS VERSUS MOTIVATING MANAGERS *(cont.)*

Demoralizing Managers	Motivating Managers
Assign projects or tasks at machine-gun speed and then disappear from the scene.	Delegate projects or tasks at a reasonable pace and take care that the team understands the assignment and has the resources to reach the goal.
Hire people they perceive to be less capable than they themselves, and spend time defining acceptable boundaries.	Hire people smarter than they are, push them to think creatively, and challenge them to grow and contribute to their full capacity.
Communicate indirectly, make assumptions about what their people know, and leave staff guessing about their standards and expectations.	Communicate their expectations directly, clearly, and confidently.
Communicate inconsistently, infrequently, and impersonally. When staff does hear from them, the communication is typically "bad news" or negative feedback.	Communicate personally, regularly, and consistently, in both good times and bad.

Demoralizing managers cost a fortune while motivating managers serve as a magnet for their organization.

Demoralizing managers cost a fortune in staff absenteeism and turnover, while motivating managers serve as a magnet for their organization. As a leader, your communication habits, attitudes, skills, and practices need to rise above the "average" and actually attract people to your team.

Make your communication practices a strategic recruitment tool. Word will travel that you're the leader to work with at the organization.

CHAPTER 14

Course-Correct Quickly After Bad Decisions

*Power is nothing unless
you can turn it into influence.*

—CONDOLEEZZA RICE, FORMER
US SECRETARY OF STATE IN THE
GEORGE W. BUSH ADMINISTRATION

Ever find yourself in an organization or on a team that's struggling because of a leader's poor decision? You sit back and reflect on the leader personally and wonder why a savvy, experienced, and ordinarily capable person could make such a dumb decision—one that wrecks a project or destroys the morale of so many people.

As a leader yourself, you may be scratching your head wondering the same thing about a past decision: Where did I go wrong? How did I miss the signs that this decision would sink the ship so fast? Analyze such situations—in your own organization along with those huge scandals in the news—and you'll find several common causes.

"BEEN THERE, DONE THAT" SYNDROME

When faced with new situations, leaders sometimes inadvertently shortcut their decision-making skills by shoving the issue into the same category as previous problems. But they have faulty memories. The situation *isn't* the same.

Blockbuster and Eastman Kodak come to mind. Confronted with a revolution in digital technology, the leadership team at Kodak refused to believe the industry really would change so dramatically. They thought they'd bury the competition like they had so many other times before. Blockbuster simply never dreamed that the video rental business was moving to a monthly subscription model—until they went bust and start-up Netflix swallowed their customer base.

Some leaders continue to think every new challenge is simply a version of an old challenge they've overcome. Result: The new problem swallows them—and sometimes their entire organization—before they realize it.

I recently discussed a problem with a senior leader; a decision he'd made was being widely ignored or circumvented throughout his organization. I suggested that he survey representatives of the various departments to get feedback on the situation and alternatives. His response: "Look, I *already know* what people will say. Anyway, you only get negative feedback on a survey."

To date, he has done nothing to right the ship, and the organization has largely ignored his directives, going around him to ask for approvals and to get things done. Currently, his ship is taking on water fast; he's climbing to a higher deck and pretending not to notice the insurrection. As I write this book, a few months later, he's fallen overboard, wondering how it all happened.

SELF-INTEREST ABOVE THE COMMON GOOD

Some savvy leaders look out for the team, department, or organization—up to a point. But when the common good clashes with what's best for them personally, the tide turns. Of course, to a degree, everyone has self-interest in mind. Otherwise, they'd never ask the salary when they accept a job, never underprice their services or product as a seller, and never expect a raise or promotion.

At question here are *inappropriate* self-interests: lying, withholding information that sabotages a project, blaming others, refusing to own up to mistakes, or taking credit for others' work or ideas.

POWER

A leadership position, however gained, grants power. And power feeds ego. Sometimes leaders begin to "believe their own press"—that they are always the smartest person in the room. These leaders surround themselves with people who continually reinforce that concept. Information comes to them sifted through sycophants. Before long, these leaders lose touch with reality. Their decisions therefore may or may not reflect the reality of a situation.

A few years ago, a general manager bragged of his resignation from an organization with an overblown sense of his own power and importance there: "Although I'm leaving for a better opportunity, in some ways I feel bad about going. So many people are upset at my resignation. I look for several of them to resign because I'm leaving."

Reality check: Nobody resigned when that general manager left. The CEO reports that the company has continued to grow without him. The perceptions of powerful people become distorted when they surround themselves with only their supporters.

HOW LEADERS
COURSE-CORRECT AND
COMMUNICATE AFTER A POOR DECISION

Accept responsibility for the faulty decision. Nothing starts you on the road to recovering trust like admitting to your troops your lapse in judgment. It's the *failure* to do so that infuriates others and compels them to keep pointing out the poor decision and its consequences. Confession is not only good for the soul but also good for clearing the record and refilling the trust account.

Hear from the troops regularly.
To stay grounded, you need information from all sources. You have to ask difficult questions—questions that may generate troubling answers. You have to deal

Nothing starts you on the **road to recovering trust** like admitting to your troops your lapse in judgment.

with perceptions. You need to understand the impact your actions, your words, and your silences have on other people. Certainly, feedback mechanisms like the 360-degree assessments work to create awareness. And punishing people for telling you hard truths is unwise.

Find confidantes. Seek out someone or a small circle of trusted confidantes *who do not report to you or depend on you for a paycheck*—an internal or external coach, mentors, a spouse, or friends. These people can help you stay focused on the tough challenges of leadership.

Smart decisions come from smart leaders committed to staying grounded in reality by communicating with a wide circle of people at all levels.

CHAPTER 15

Develop Your People

Leadership and learning are indispensable to each other.

—JOHN F. KENNEDY,
FORMER US PRESIDENT

After my keynote to his organization, the CEO of a large import-export company invited me to dinner. In discussing my late-night departure from the Florida venue, we swapped a few stories about the difficulty of getting information from airlines about flight delays. Immediately, his eyes widened, and his face reddened at the mention of one particular airline.

"I absolutely refuse to use that airline any longer for our shipments!" he said. "Their lying got to be ridiculous. I'd ask if my shipment was going to be put on a certain flight. The agent accepting the shipment would say yes. But then I'd get a call from my customer in Brazil, saying the shipment didn't make it. . . . Sure enough, I'd check with the airline agent and discover the shipment never got on the flight."

As I listened to him, remembering my own misrouted luggage, I felt his pain.

The CEO continued, "Finally, I found a platform agent I could trust.

No matter what the check-in agent told me, I'd walk around to the dock and ask *that* specific agent directly if my shipment was really going to make it onto the plane. He'd give me an honest answer. If no, then I could call my client in Brazil and tell him the shipment wasn't going to make it onto the plane. . . . I could always count on that employee to tell me the truth."

I nodded again. "You need people like that."

The CEO went on, "When they [that airline] laid off people about three years after that, I hired that agent. Didn't even have a job for him then. But I want people like that on my staff—people who tell the truth. He's bilingual, a quick learner. I knew I'd find a place for him and groom him. He's made a great employee."

Straight from the lips of a strategic thinker who understands the value of scouting for talent. I've never forgotten this conversation from early in my career. And I've heard many similar stories since from senior executives.

But according to a PricewaterhouseCoopers survey and a Korn Ferry Institute study by researcher Robert Eichinger, most managers lag far behind in developing themselves and their people. The "ability to grow talent" is ranked 67th out of 67 identified competencies for managers![7]

So what happens when employees discover that personal development doesn't show up on their supervisor's priority list? They leave. According to a recent Harris Poll of more than 2,000 employees, roughly one-third (32 percent) of adult employees in the United States reported that they were currently planning to leave their job for lack of career development. And 55 percent of those working full-time and part-time expect their company to play an active role in their individual career options.[8]

But wait. Personal development doesn't necessarily mean handholding and time off the job for training.

Old-school thinking meant one-size-fits-all training. Design training courses. Send your staff. Wait for them to come back equipped to do the job. Then that process evolved into segmenting "high-potentials" into a separate track for stretch assignments, special mentoring, and extra exposure to the executive movers and shakers to hear their thinking on strategic issues and challenges. Again, most of these drills involved one-way communication—as in, "Here's what we think you need to know."

Today's employees, however, expect to be *heard*—they want *personalized* career development that fits their goals, dreams, plans, and lifestyle. They expect their leaders to show interest in their career (beyond simply getting their current job done) and either coach or advise them on how to reach their potential.[9] In fact, more quickly than they leave a boring party, millennials drop an employer when they see no career-growth opportunities. And after 2020, according to researchers who study population shifts, millennials will comprise more than 51 percent of the US workforce.[10]

Study after study confirms that career development has become *the* cool calling card. It's a powerful opening act to tease job seekers to join your organization or team.

> Today's **employees expect**
> to be *heard*—they want **personalized**
> career development that fits their
> goals, dreams, plans, and lifestyle.

Leaders know all this. They believe all this. They actually want these career-development opportunities for themselves.

So what's the problem? In a fast-paced, understaffed, deadline-driven atmosphere, developing team members simply falls to the bottom of the leader's to-do list. Supervisors say they're so busy that they have no time to think about what they consider "extra" benefits and needs.

As a strategic thinker, though, you'll keep bringing career conversations to the forefront with individual team members and coworkers. Let them know you're interested in their development and in their long-term career advancement. The once-a-year performance appraisal session (if you still have those) does not do the topic justice—nor does it demonstrate the priority the topic deserves.

Here's how to let colleagues and your own team members know you care about their career and their personal growth opportunities.

> More quickly than they leave a boring party, **millennials** drop an employer when they see **no career-growth opportunities**.

Reconfirm their interests for future assignments and career growth on an ongoing basis. Ask about changes in immediate and long-term goals. New skills gained? New stretch assignments they'd like to take on? Hobbies become career aspirations. Career aspirations fade to become only hobby interests. Income and savings goals evolve as the family situation changes. Health issues necessitate lifestyle and career changes. Simply asking to update yourself on current needs, desires, and priorities demonstrates interest.

Look for a mentoring moment. You may not have an hour to devote to your team member, but you can spare a minute or ten. When the occasion arises, call that interested team member to "join me on a conference call at two o'clock if you're interested in learning what's involved in X." Or invite them to "step into my office for a minute. I just decided to sign a contract with Z Company. Let me tell you how I arrived at that decision, so in the future when these things come up, you'll have some background here." The individual will understand that you are investing time—no matter how brief—in their career development.

Suggest resources, and make team members accountable for their own development. The resources may be your own HR function, a local university, industry conferences, books, audios, subscription programs, webinars, or online training programs. Whatever they choose, make sure your team members understand that they own the responsibility for their development in the same way they own responsibility for their physical fitness. Simply point out the resource that you've discovered, and suggest that they may want to investigate its value further for their own purposes.

Then don't forget to follow up. Later, ask if they found the resource helpful. What did they like or not like? Did they find another book, course, or app more useful?

Reinforce career growth every chance you get. At staff meetings, as part of your discussions from time to time, ask what team members need to learn. Bring in either internal or external experts to address these issues. Report to the group on new things you're learning: concepts from articles, blog posts, and books you've read; ideas from conferences you've attended; insights you've picked up from mentors. Ask what new skills they've mastered and suggest they report these updates to HR for their employee file. When discussing individual action plans, be sure to ask about their career development specifics.

Make learning a topic of casual discussion. A couple of friends of mine who are master networkers routinely ask at parties, "So, what's become clearer to you since the last time we talked?" That canned cocktail-party opening can easily be modified for mentoring purposes: "What new learning opportunities have you been able to take advantage of since we last talked about your career?" Allow time in staff meetings occasionally (and with prior notice) for a few to mention a learning resource (blog, book, podcast, course) they have found helpful and would recommend to their coworkers.

For example, several companies use my books for discussion in Lunch-N-Learn peer-to-peer personal development programs and for internal business book reading clubs. (You can download the free Discussion Guide we've provided for this purpose at www.Communicate LikeALeaderBook.com.) Audience members at industry conferences often take notes and handouts back to team members to share at the next staff meeting.

All of these opportunities, if encouraged by a department leader, demonstrate interest in career development for the team and for individuals. Millennials particularly thrive on feedback and interest in their career growth.

Again, such casual discussions accomplish several purposes beyond demonstrating interest: they keep you up to date on changes in employee goals, reinforce that team members themselves own the responsibility for their personal development, and provide opportunity for a mentoring moment or two from you or more experienced group members. And you, as leader, have facilitated that learning.

Scouting talent and developing your team (or coworkers) doesn't mean spending a massive chunk of time at the tail end of an already packed month. This strategic conversation can be brief but powerfully engaging. After all, who doesn't like to talk about themselves and their future career opportunities?

PART 2

STRATEGIC CONVERSATIONS
Connect With Intent

*How, when, and where you say something can
actually be more important than the message itself.*

—ANNE BRUCE AND JAMES S. PEPITONE,
BUSINESS AUTHORS AND CONSULTANTS

*Discussion is an exchange of knowledge;
argument an exchange of ignorance.*

—ROBERT QUILLEN, HUMORIST
AND JOURNALIST

*To be able to ask a question clearly is
two-thirds of the way to getting it answered.*

—JOHN RUSKIN, 19TH-CENTURY
ENGLISH ARTIST AND ART CRITIC

CHAPTER 16

Be Intentional About Your Communication Standards

The challenge of leadership is to be strong, but
not rude; be kind, but not weak; be bold, but not a bully;
be thoughtful, but not lazy; be humble, but not timid;
be proud, but not arrogant; have humor, but without folly.

—JIM ROHN, ENTREPRENEUR,
AUTHOR, AND MOTIVATIONAL SPEAKER

Ask any marketing expert the definition of branding, and they'll tell you that branding is not what you do for yourself. It's what your customers or coworkers think when they think of you. You create your personal communication "brand" day by day over time as you interact with your staff, colleagues, and executives within and outside your organization. What comes to mind when others think of how you interact with them? Circle descriptors that you think might pop into someone's mind when they consider you and your communication style.

YOUR BRANDED COMMUNICATION STYLE

Positives	Negatives	Positives	Negatives
Truthful	Deceptive	Precise	Vague
Responsive	Unresponsive	Careful	Careless
Warm, cordial	Distant, cold	Accurate	Inaccurate, wrong
Tactful	Blunt	Energetic	Lazy
Concise	Verbose	Emotionally stable	Emotionally unstable
Humble	Arrogant	Logical	Illogical
Sense of humor	Humorless	Intriguing	Boring
Knowledgeable	Clueless	Engaged	Disengaged
Resourceful	Inept	Witty, clever	Dull
Insightful	Dense	Courteous	Rude
Provocative	Tedious	Compassionate	Uncaring
Trusting	Cynical	Sensitive	Insensitive
Gracious	Sarcastic	Intelligent	Dumb, slow

Your communication "brand" is determined by all of your personal interactions stacked end to end.

When you examine your personal list of modifiers, is that the impression or brand you intend to create? Most people think they communicate well. Yet given the current political unrest, racial tensions, international conflicts, workplace disengagement, and divorce rate, how can so many people insist they are skilled at communication? Needless to say, we can all work toward improving clarity, connection, influence, inspiration, and impact.

Although few would claim to be a master communicator in all these arenas, we *can* learn to be intentional in our communication at home, work, and elsewhere by establishing for ourselves communication standards. Think of these "best practices" that you might follow for any job:

Strong communicators understand the strategic importance of* always *telling the truth. Telling the truth—without twisting the timeline, adding or omitting information, editorializing, distorting facts, or otherwise misrepresenting a situation—becomes the foundation for all interactions between two people. Truth-telling is the circuitry for trust. When that connection is broken, there's no basis for further attempts to communicate.

Strong communicators listen for strategic opportunities and avoid minefields. They know what's inside their *own* head. The goal is to understand what's inside the head of another person. When you're always in "talk" mode, you'll always be at a disadvantage, knowing only what you yourself think or intend. Listening (not simply hearing) benefits strong communicators several ways: You demonstrate interest in the other party, you learn, and you can respond appropriately.

Strong communicators read body language for the complete message. Words are never the whole story. Meaning is conveyed in tone of voice, volume, facial expression,

> **Truth-telling** is the **circuitry for trust**. When that connection is broken, there's no basis for further attempts to **communicate**.

eye contact or the lack thereof, smiling, nodding, gestures, handshake, and posture. All of these things and more tell you how someone *feels* about the topic of discussion or their presentation.

Strong communicators choose precise words for strategic messages. Reckless writing and speaking detract from the primary concerns. Careful communicators eliminate "hot words" (*unfair, unreasonable, disapproval, complaint, disgruntled*) so as not to elicit an emotional reaction to improper language.

> **Not:** "Stemco always seems *disgruntled* and *unreasonable* about such clauses in our contracts, extending our negotiations for weeks; in my opinion, we should drop them from the bidders list and go with a company that has fairer pricing."

> **But:** "Negotiations with Stemco on the last three contracts have extended for weeks; I'd like to remove them from our bidders list and work with a company more in line with our initial pricing."

Strong communicators pay attention to emotional context. They understand how the listener's mindset positively or negatively affects how someone translates a message. So they make sure to select the appropriate emotional backdrop against which to deliver sensitive news.

For example, let's say your company has gone through a merger in the last 60 days, but you have no plans for massive layoffs. Also, let's say that you need to talk with your team about a new competitor just entering the market and gaining market share. As you mention "cost-cutting measures" to remain competitive in light of this new start-up, if you are not specific about the meaning of that phrase, your team will quite likely think you're referring to layoffs as a result of the merger. That emotional backdrop overlays your words.

Strategic communicators understand the importance of timing. They're not going to ask for a raise immediately after learning that the stock price has fallen 35 percent. Nor will they give a briefing about losing their biggest client half an hour before making a big sales call with a new prospect.

> Words
> are never **the**
> **whole story**.

Strong communicators understand how confidentiality aids persuasion. They know that people feel pressure to say things they don't mean when egos become involved. For example, Marco speaks up in a meeting to support Solution A to a problem. Three other colleagues in the room agree with him. Kevin debates the issue, saying he wholeheartedly disagrees with Solution A. Marco solidly restates his position for Solution A, although he cannot express his reasons as articulately as Kevin. Kevin again refutes Marco's position, clearly noting his own position and reasons for Solution B. The three onlookers, who originally agreed with Marco, now look baffled. And if Kevin persists in disagreeing, he seems defiant and disgruntled.

Both Marco and Kevin will find it difficult to persist in their opinions for two reasons. The disagreement has become public, and onlookers must take a "side" for winners and losers.

Winning will now involve ego, because a person is attached to each solution—Marco's solution and Kevin's solution.

Grandstanding typically has a detrimental effect on persuasion. Had Marco and Kevin chosen to discuss the matter privately, they might have come to agreement more easily. But as the situation stands, the discussion has become a battle of egos—winner take all. Deciding to discuss a controversial issue confidentially takes leadership.

Any *one* of these seven communication practices can increase your influence. Be intentional as you focus on them. Adopting *all* seven will play a strategic role in your success as a leader.

CHAPTER 17

Be a Leader
Who Laughs

Next to power without honor,
the most dangerous thing in the world
is power without humor.

—ERIC SEVAREID,
JOURNALIST

The first day I walked into Miss Amos's literature class, I was scared. Not because of the subject or the fact that this was my first day in a new school—I was frightened by her face.

I took my seat and slid around to look at her squarely. Her large nose curved sharply toward her left cheekbone. Big, dark bags hung under piercing eyes. Her cheeks sunk in and then exploded into an oddly shaped, oversized mouth. Her silver hair was parted perfectly straight and combed flat down to her ears, then was held in place by a tight row of pin curls around the edges. Below her neck, everything else seemed normal in her smartly tailored dress.

She turned to the board behind her and wrote silently in bold print: *MISS AMOS*. Turning back to face us, she said dryly, "You'll notice there's no period after the *Miss*. That makes it all too final. I'm still hoping."

The class laughed uneasily, and that began my junior year with Miss Amos and her wry sense of humor.

A student sauntered into class late one day, mumbling apologies about oversleeping. Miss Amos harrumphed, and tartly said, "Chris, if you're sleeping more than three hours a night, you're sleeping your life away. At age eighteen, do you know how much of your life you've already missed?" Chris slid into his seat sheepishly. But as Miss Amos surveyed the room with her sardonic smile, the comment was not lost on the rest of us. (Nor, apparently, was it lost on Chris, for that matter. He became a state senator.)

By late November, her huge bulletin board bulged with mums and green ribbons, each sprouting a football player's glittering number. Two days before the homecoming game, the bulletin board had mums three rows deep inside the flowered frame. Her explanation? Former students sent them "just because."

Miss Amos never walked onto a football field, basketball court, or running track. But her classroom trained more athletes in leadership than many coaches do in a lifetime. She taught us to read broadly, think deeply, speak thoughtfully, write clearly, and persuade artfully—mostly through the use of humor wrapped around a heart of love. By May, I hardly noticed her face anymore. I'm guessing most other students forgot about it also. Miss Amos has a school named after her now.

As a leader and influencer, you too have a choice about how you deal with stress to accomplish a mission with your team.

GET UPSET OR GET A LAUGH

Humor hides a multitude of unattractive physical features, petty habits, and personality quirks that might otherwise irritate people. With the pressures of leadership, you have a choice—to get upset or to get a laugh. Getting upset boosts your blood pressure; laughing and a lighthearted culture boosts your productivity and your influence.

Around our training company, when the workload peaked and the pressure mounted, we could always count on Dr. Einstein of Grammar to relieve the tension.

After Random House released the paperback version of my earlier grammar book, a guy called our receptionist, identifying himself as the Dr. Einstein of Grammar. "I just finished reading Dianna's grammar book and found numerous grammatical errors. Astounding that such a reputable publisher would release a book with so many incorrect rules and examples. I need to speak to the author to make her aware of all the errors!"

"She's out of town today," the receptionist told him. "But I'm sure she'd like to know. Can you tell me what errors you've found so I can pass them along to her?"

"Everywhere. The rules are wrong throughout the book! *That*. *Which*. Quotation marks. *Who*. *Whom*. Capitalization."

"Hmmm. Well, I'll let her know. In the meantime, why don't you email a few items to me and I'll pass them along to Dianna and the publisher?"

"I'll do that!"

(Despite many proofreadings, authors and publishers do make mistakes, and they want to know so they can correct errors in future printings.)

Dr. Einstein of Grammar sent his email—chockful of his *own* grammatical errors, typos, and misspellings. His sentences were so convoluted that it was difficult to follow his points. Clearly, he was no grammarian. The receptionist passed his email around the office, and the admin staff enjoyed a good laugh about his moniker.

For months, Dr. Einstein of Grammar repeatedly called our office, demanding to speak to me so he could "set me straight." And for months, when a client called with a technical writing question that stumped the admin staff, someone in the office would invariably say, "Why don't you check with Dr. Einstein of Grammar?" The response never failed to lighten the mood in the office.

> Getting **upset** boosts your blood pressure; laughing and a lighthearted culture **boosts your productivity and your influence**.

Humor helps relieve tension. It may only take a second. And it may last for years. So if you want to increase your influence as a leader, add more humor to your conversations and your workplace.

GUIDELINES FOR PUTTING HUMOR INTO PLAY

- Test your own motives in your use of humor toward others. Genuine humor leaves no sting. Never disguise a "message" to someone in a humorous barb. Remember that sarcasm reflects the lowest form of humor. Humor should strengthen and heal—not weaken and hurt—relationships. If the humor makes someone uncomfortable, it's inappropriate.

- Look for the positive in negative situations.

- Respond in a lighthearted rather than heavy-handed way to tension in relationships.

- Take an easygoing approach to brainstorming and problem solving in discussions or meetings. Permit time for a joke or a laugh; humor releases tension in even the most serious situation and allows people to continue to work under extreme pressure.

- Consider your word choices carefully in sensitive situations. Use the tactful, positive, or neutral word rather than the potentially offensive or negative phrasing.

- Learn how to tell a good story or anecdote to illustrate your points—even in formal business presentations or business meetings.

- Take care when putting humor in writing. A lighthearted comment said with a smile and a pat on the back often comes across differently on the screen or the page. At best, the comment may not be funny; at worst, it may offend.

- Learn to laugh at yourself. Understand that your reputation, respect, ego, career, or future is not on the line with every mistake, decision, or circumstance that develops.

- Practice a little self-deprecating humor in front of others— admit a few mistakes, errors in judgment, or wrong decisions by telling funny stories on yourself. You'll likely see that others' opinions of you rise rather than fall. Their admiration and appreciation will likely grow because of your willingness to be vulnerable.

- Give others permission to laugh at your mistakes without malice. When someone cracks a joke or delivers a one-liner at your expense, rather than be defensive, enjoy the humor yourself. Others take their cue from you. Assume no ill will unless you have proof that the person actually meant to embarrass you. (When that's the case, talk with the jokester privately about the underlying cause.)

To paraphrase an old German proverb, "A person shows their character by what they find funny—or not." Laughter engages, connects, and expands your influence as a leader.

Humor hides a multitude of unattractive physical features, petty habits, and personality quirks that might otherwise irritate people.
    With the pressures of leadership, you have a choice—to get upset or to get a laugh.

CHAPTER 18

Respond Promptly in the Age of Twitter

*Leaders who make it a practice to draw out the
thoughts and ideas of their subordinates and who
are receptive even to bad news will be properly informed.
Communicate downward to subordinates with at
least the same care and attention as you communicate
upward to superiors.*

—L. B. BELKER, INSURANCE
EXECUTIVE AND AUTHOR

Ninety-six percent of current smartphone owners say they rarely or never shut off their phones. Users expect to be in touch constantly with friends, family, or colleagues on social media.[11] With unlimited texting and tools and new apps entering the marketplace like popcorn, people can schedule their memes and messages to land every twenty to thirty minutes.

On social media, the expectation time for response is zero to four hours. How fast do companies typically respond? Ten hours, according to various studies by social media experts and bloggers. Big disappointment.

But more to the point here: Is it any wonder that coworkers and customers expect prompt responses to emails and texts? Yet a Gallup poll of 1,000 German employees revealed that only 60 percent strongly agreed that their manager responds to calls or messages within 24 hours.[12] So roughly 40 percent must sit in a "holding pattern" on the current project, waiting for an answer.

Have you yourself ever waited and waited for a response from your boss before moving forward on a project or decision? If so, you understand the drag on productivity. Team members want acknowledgment that you've received a key report or proposal and that you'll respond shortly with approval, a no-go, or a request for more information.

You as team leader need to communicate clearly to your team what the standard response time is for your team: 4 hours? 8 hours? 24 hours? Are there exceptions to this standard? If so, what? Once you've communicated the standard, live by it.

Slow responses suggest many things—most of them negative:

- You're overwhelmed and can't keep up with the pace.

- You're puzzled by the decision or action required.

- Your system of handling daily inquiries is ineffective.

- You have a staffing problem.

- The situation, decision, or project is unimportant to you.

- You need time to deliberate before replying.

- You need to gather more information or input before responding.

A big part of strategic thinking involves sorting the significant from the trivial, putting efficient systems in place to handle routine matters, and prioritizing the important over the urgent.

A common time-management mistake for less effective communicators is to handle "urgent" matters before important matters. They define those "urgent" matters as those with a deadline—no matter how unimportant they might be, matters like reserving ad space, returning a phone call, replying to a colleague's request for information. However, when there are too many "urgent" matters, that leader never gets the truly important things done. Finishing ONE high-priority important project may contribute more value than completing seven "urgent" tasks.

Granted, speed can lead to poor decisions based on missing or faulty data. When you need more time to reflect, simply acknowledge to the sender that you've received their message and that you'll reply fully later or by X date.

Speed has become the newest metric of quality communication. The second phase: Prioritizing important tasks over urgent tasks. The third phase: Increasing the speed of handling both your important communication *and* the urgent. Everything needs to be acknowledged and dispatched in some way.

Little misses can lead to big losses.

> **Speed**
> has become
> the **newest metric** of
> quality communication.

CHAPTER 19

Learn to **Apologize** or **Pay** the Penalty

*When you realize you've made a mistake,
make amends immediately. It's easier to
eat crow while it's still warm.*

—DAN HEIST, FICTIONAL CHARACTER
IN A DANIEL SILVA MOVIE

If the public can learn anything from politicians, professional athletes, and celebrities, it's this: When you make a mistake, apologize promptly and sincerely. With an apology, those who love you will forgive you. Without an apology, those who don't love you will not relent until they track you to the ends of the earth and drain every ounce of energy.

When individuals or organizations refuse to apologize for a mistake, bad judgment, or other offense, they will inevitably pay a penalty in bad PR. Any situation can go viral in a matter of minutes. And even if they do eventually apologize, the delay simply creates doubt: Is this a heartfelt apology, or did they buckle under pressure?

During my training program on customer service communication years ago, a manager in the audience at a large oil company commented, "They don't allow us to apologize specifically around here." Because he had earlier identified himself as supervisor of the division that wrote all the responses from their customer service department, I probed further.

According to his boss, this manager most definitely had *not* been given that direction; it was not company policy to refrain from offering apologies and accepting responsibility for errors. The direction from the senior legal team had been to take care that he did not assume *legal liability* in a situation involving injury or loss without consulting with the legal team. However, this manager's comment reveals a common misunderstanding about apologies: An apology does *not* mean you are accepting responsibility for *causing* a problem. An apology can simply mean you regret a situation, an event, or an outcome.

To be effective, an apology should be swift, sincere, specific, and solution-focused.

Swift. If people are calling for an apology, it's probably overdue. The blunder has attracted attention beyond the original point of pain (personal, group, organization, customer), and that in and of itself means it has gone viral. The faster you apologize, the faster the grapevine will have something to carry besides the original offense.

Sincere. Humility beats arrogance every time. If you don't understand the problem or pain, investigate. Find the facts. Hear the other person or party describe what has happened from their viewpoint. While you may state that the slight or offense was unintended, acknowledge the other party's perspective.

Specific. Never reach into your apology template and pull out a statement like "I apologize for any inconvenience this may have caused you." Or "Thank you for your patience as we investigate this matter." The first statement minimizes the issue. "Inconvenience?" "*May* have caused you?" Both phrases suggest that the speaker/writer is downplaying the incident. The second statement (*Thanks for your patience*) takes a breezy air, assuming that the other party is patient. Neither phrasing demonstrates specific acknowledgment of a problem or an understanding of the trouble caused.

Both statements sound as though someone has suggested to a subordinate, "Why not give these people the bug-in-the-pickle-juice apology email? Or, better yet, let's try the sorry-you-leaned-against-the-freshly-painted-wall template. That apology should do fine—just change the address and signature block."

Be specific about *what* happened and *why* it happened. If you're still investigating, say so and state when you'll report further information.

Solution-focused. The message of primary interest to the other person or party will be what you intend to do to correct the problem. Often, the only correction is an admission of fault, insensitivity, oversight, or error. Swallow your pride, own up to the mistake, and offer your sincere regrets. Other occasions may call for concrete amends. Offer to reschedule the meeting, renegotiate a deadline, reword the offensive email, give an extra discount to your distributor on the disputed order, provide temporary workers from your department to cover the worker shortage, set up a meeting to discuss the issue, or make an introduction to someone else in a position to help.

Just do something to make it right.

Sometimes keeping a strategic partnership or internal client relationship intact revolves around your ability to say you're sorry—specifically, sincerely, swiftly—with a solution.

CHAPTER 20

Keep Your
Networks Active

*The currency of real networking
is not greed but generosity.*

—KEITH FERRAZZI,
AUTHOR AND CONSULTANT

Chances are you've returned from a party, networking event, trade show, or conference with a handful of business cards, spread them across your desk, and asked yourself, "Now who was this person? And why do I care?"

You don't want to fall in that category for someone else. Your challenge: Stand out from the crowd so others recall your conversation and remember you as a strategic connection from the get-go so that when you need to call on them with a question, they know who you are. How difficult is that?

You might want to test your own recall. Consider the last three networking opportunities you've attended as you answer the following questions. By networking opportunities, I'm referring to events that you chose to attend for the express purpose of intermingling with like-minded professionals—whether to discuss a topic, celebrate an event, learn something new, hear a speaker, or present your own product or service. The event might have been a trade show, an industry conference, a civic meeting, or a holiday party.

- Estimate the total number of people who attended all three events. _____

- Of that total number, how many people can you recall meeting personally? _____

- Of the people you met personally, how many people can you still name? _____

- Of the people you can still recall by name, how many could you recall well enough to refer them to an interested customer, supplier, or friend for potential work? _____

If your answer to the last question is "Not many," then you understand the real difficulty of making yourself memorable to others and keeping your network active.

WHY KEEP YOUR NETWORK ACTIVE?

Salespeople know they bring more to the negotiating table than their sales skills. In fact, financial advisors often speak of the "book of business" they'll be bringing to a new employer, as if they had their clients packed in their briefcase. In the workplace, whether in sales, HR, or engineering, your professional network represents a key asset to both you and your organization.

The benefits to you *personally* include:

- Resources in the industry to validate and discuss new trends

- Recommendations for suppliers who perform consistently at a reasonable price when you don't have time to go through a long vetting process

- Recruitment of the best job candidates

- Referrals on equipment, software, and project management processes that others have tested and that you need to put into use quickly

- Referrals on quality training or speakers

- Quick answers to questions when you don't have time to go through "proper" channels

- Job searches when you're ready to make a move—either internally or externally

Second, your network benefits your *organization*. The more you can "work your network" for information and leads, the more money you save your employer. No matter what position you hold, your organization expects you to keep your network active.

WHO TO INCLUDE IN YOUR NETWORK

That depends on you and where you work, of course. But most professionals will want and need these people in their network:

— Industry experts or consultants in and out of other organizations

— Counterparts in other departments/divisions/regions

— Suppliers who service your industry

— Friendly competitors

— Contacts at client organizations (three deep—your contact, your contact's boss, your contact's boss's boss)

— Contacts at your own organization two levels above you and two levels below you

— A technology specialist

— A marketing specialist

— A social media specialist

— An attorney (generalist)

— An intellectual property attorney

— A financial advisor

— A CPA and a tax specialist

— A Realtor®

— A physician

— A spiritual counselor

You'll notice that this list gets personal toward the end (IP attorney through spiritual counselor). You'll need these people in your network for decisions that arise about ethics, health, investing, compensation structures, investment opportunities, stress reduction, personal relationships, and life balance. All of these personal concerns obviously affect your work life.[13]

HOW TO KEEP YOUR NETWORK ACTIVE

Having names in your database or cell phone does *not* equate to keeping people *active* in your network. The question becomes, Will these people take your call at 7:00 a.m.—or at least return your call or email within 48 hours? If not, consider them inactive. So how do you keep them from going inactive?

- **Serve.** Give of your time. Get involved so your name is on people's minds. Volunteer for committees. Go to work for a charitable cause.

- **Become a resource.** Send along articles or links to blogs, books, or ezine subscriptions in specialty niches they may not be aware of on topics of interest. Provide data that you think would interest them.

- **Provide introductions.** Two colleagues of mine pass along an introduction to me at least once a month—someone they think would benefit from my coaching on executive presence or book writing and marketing. And they pass on such introductions for others as well. For them, "cyber-introductions" have become a habit.

> Will these people take your call at 7:00 a.m.—or at least return your call or email within 48 hours? **If not**, consider them inactive.

- **Be a sounding board.** Occasionally, call to ask what's going on and then listen, show sincere interest, and offer ideas. Phone calls have become a rarity today, and people appreciate the attention—as long as the attention is for the other person's benefit, not yours.

YOUR BIGGEST DANGER: DECLINING VALUE

Bank accounts, according to federal law, go dormant if no transactions occur during a three-year period, and the assets are turned over to the state. For lack of a little activity, your portfolio value declines dramatically to zero.

Likewise, for lack of a little activity, your portfolio of contacts can lose some or all of its value. How do you know when your network has begun to decline?

- Fewer calls for your advice or opinion

- Fewer requests for introductions to others

- Decreasing social media engagement

- No references by peers to your comments (not being quoted here or there in meetings)

- Fewer requests to present sessions or participate on panels at industry conferences

- Fewer guest invitations to community or industry events or celebrations

- Fewer media requests

As these contacts grow more and more scarce, fewer and fewer people hear your name linked to your area of expertise. As people leave their organization to join other firms, you gradually lose connection to your network for information, top talent, and industry trends.

Leaders understand the strategic importance of an active personal network. Maintain meaningful communication to keep your network strong, expand its reach, and increase its value.

PART 3

STRATEGIC NEGOTIATIONS
Look for Mutual Opportunities

In business as in life, you don't get what you deserve, you get what you negotiate.

—CHESTER L. KARRASS,
NEGOTIATIONS EXPERT AND AUTHOR

Ask often and ask outrageously!
The worst you can hear is,
"No" or "Not now."

—LINDA SWINDLING,
AUTHOR, ATTORNEY, AND
NEGOTIATIONS EXPERT

You must be fully prepared to lose a great deal in order to make a great deal.

—UNKNOWN

CHAPTER 21

Determine Your Goals, Value, and Walk-Away Point

The fellow who says he'll meet you halfway
usually thinks he's standing on the dividing line.

—ORLANDO A. BATTISTA,
CHEMIST AND AUTHOR

We negotiate every day in our personal lives and at work: interpersonal disagreements, project or delivery deadlines, travel and vacation packages, discounts on damaged goods, mortgage or rent rates, salary increases, job responsibilities, and household duties. Many such negotiations are routine and don't require much strategic thinking. Others demand serious forethought because the outcome may lock you into consequences for a long time. When the stakes matter, do your prep before any serious discussions begin.

Step 1: Identify your primary, long-term goal. Are you trying to set up a strategic partnership with organization A to distribute all your products?

Do you want authorization to increase head count in your department by three during the next year? Do you want the company to pay for a three-month sabbatical while you finish an off-site training program?

As you identify your primary, long-term goal, you may notice that some goals are easy to measure (increase price by 15 percent over the next two years) while others are more nebulous (improve customer satisfaction). With difficult-to-measure goals, it helps to set ranges: What's the best outcome you can hope to achieve? What's the least improvement in your situation that you'll consider a success?

Step 2: Identify your immediate goal. Before you can accomplish your long-term goal, make sure you can get to first base. Determine any interim steps. Be as specific as possible. If your goal is to snag the XYZ organization as a regular client for all your health-care supplies, an interim goal might be to get at least an order for *one* of your health-care product lines.

Step 3: Identify your nice-to-have goals. Consider other things you plan to ask for during your negotiation that would be of value to you. Often, the other party is pleased to trade away things that have little or no value to them. However, remember that, as you request these things, the other party—if they are a skilled negotiator—will keep track of them and ask for trades in return.

Step 4: Determine the value of what you can offer. Make a list of things (tangibles and intangibles) that may or may not have much value to you but that the other party may consider very valuable. Of course, you will have to research the other party to determine what they might value. (Examples: personal time with executives, faster delivery time, better guarantee, customized feature, no upfront payment requirement, final report on your work.) Be ready to offer these "concessions" in kind for valuable concessions you want from the other party.

Step 5: Decide on your walk-away point. Never enter a negotiation feeling as though you *must* come to agreement. If you do, you lose. Negotiating from a position of desperation only leads into a sinkhole. Before you open your mouth, know what you consider acceptable terms. When the discussion moves beyond that point, be comfortable with walking away until another day—or another opportunity comes along.

Consider this example of the five steps. Let's say your company wants to hire a consulting firm to "create a communication plan" for an upcoming conference for your prospects flying in from around the world to hear updates on your newest products and services. The consulting firm will need to prepare and train all your subject-matter experts to design and deliver their various keynotes and breakout sessions for your three-day marketing conference.

Step 1: Identify your primary, long-term goal.

— Have our industry experts deliver excellent content in an engaging way at our annual three-day lead-generating marketing conference.

Step 2: Identify your immediate goal.

— Contract with the most qualified communication consulting firm to help our speakers design, prepare, and deliver their keynotes and breakout sessions in a variety of formats and styles to create a unique learning and sales experience for conference attendees.

— Get the consulting firm to assign the most qualified consultants to our project.

Step 3: Identify your nice-to-have goals.

— Negotiate a reasonable price.

— Ask that the firm's principal consultants be assigned to our project.

— Ask the firm to survey our prospects before the project
begins.

Step 4: Determine the value of what you can offer.

— Be flexible on conference dates and training dates for the
subject-matter experts (which allows them to schedule work
in their off-peak season).

— Have our own staff handle admin at our own venue, which
eliminates many of the coordination details the consultants
typically must handle (saving them 10 to 15 admin hours).

Step 5: Decide on your walk-away point.

— The maximum budget for the entire project is $75,000.

— Our staff must approve the consultants assigned.

Planning may not take much paperwork—but it does take thought.

Failure to do prep work leads to disappointing discussions. A little forethought can make all the difference in successful negotiations.

CHAPTER 22

Adopt Strategic Negotiation Practices

*During a negotiation, it would be wise not
to take anything personally. If you leave
personalities out of it, you will be able to
see opportunities more objectively.*

—BRIAN KOSLOW, INTERNATIONAL
BUSINESSMAN AND INVESTOR

Strategic negotiators stand out from their less-successful colleagues.
The following communication habits will increase your chances to
negotiate beneficial partnerships, close bigger client contracts, gain significant promotions, and resolve troublesome conflicts.

Strategic negotiators listen to a complete thought expressed. Their less-
successful colleagues assume they know what the other person is driving at, so they interrupt often, missing much of the message.

Strategic negotiators practice focused attention. Their less successful coworkers often set themselves up for failure. They become easily dis-

tracted with electronic gadgets or passersby. Trying to multi-task, they let their mind wander off topic—again missing key information that would be helpful to the discussion.

Strategic negotiators take notes on what they hear. The less-successful assume they will remember what they hear and seldom write down information for later reference.

Strategic negotiators listen for alignment. Unsuccessful negotiators tend to listen for disagreement and attempt to talk the other party over to their side. They view the discussion as an "us" versus "them" situation, with persuasion as the main tool in their toolbox.

Strategic negotiators identify opportunities—mutual acquaintances, referrals, recommendations—to make assessments and look for mutual benefit in other ventures. The successful set their radar to intercept signals from all directions. Their less-successful colleagues either fail to pick up on these tidbits of information or tune them out as irrelevant. Their radar operates on a very limited range.

Strategic negotiators ask probing questions to understand the other person's goals, needs, concerns, and resistance to an agreement. Less-successful negotiators focus on stating and restating their *own* needs, goals, and concerns, considering the other person's goals an afterthought.

Strategic negotiators let the other party make the first request or offer. The conventional wisdom is, "The person who mentions money first loses." If the other party seems reluctant to mention money first, you might elicit an offer with questions or statements: "What had you planned to pay for something like this?" "Do you have a budget in mind for this project?" "What have you paid for this service in the past?" "What's the going rate for something like this?" "Have you checked around for prices?" "What kind of financial arrangements did you have in mind?"

If your negotiation involves requests other than financial, you still might encourage the party to make their request first. "When were you thinking you could have this project completed?" "So are you aiming for any critical deadline to have this delivered?" "Are we working around any crucial supply difficulties?"

The less effective negotiator operates under the philosophy, "Let's just get this deal done (or situation handled). Take it or leave it."

Strategic negotiators avoid getting blinded by big numbers. They adequately break down the numbers and assess needs and potential opportunities over the long term. But hefty lump sums dazzle less-savvy negotiators who aren't used to assessing long-term risks and rewards.

> **Strategic negotiators** listen for alignment. **Unsuccessful negotiators** tend to listen for disagreement and attempt to talk the other party over to their side.

Strategic negotiators focus on a few key things they really want. Less-effective negotiators get caught up in the details and nickel-and-dime about unimportant matters. As a result, they walk away with a long but trivial list of "points scored."

Strategic negotiators refuse to fall for the "no exceptions" line. They understand everything is negotiable—for a price. Unskilled negotiators often accept this "no exceptions" comment and fail to ask for what they need or want.

Strategic negotiators ask questions to clarify understanding before drawing conclusions. The less successful jump to conclusions based on assumptions of what the other person wants, needs, has, or can or can't do.

Strategic negotiators read body language well. They also acknowledge that they're listening (with eye contact, facial expression, and note taking). Less-experienced negotiators pay less attention to body language—their own or the other person's. The less experienced focus primarily on words, often missing much of the real message about potential areas for a change in position or common ground.

Strategic negotiators are comfortable with silence; they listen far more than they talk. Unseasoned negotiators become rattled by silence. They talk more than they listen, giving away far too much information and failing to gather information they need to make offers or solid decisions.

Strategic negotiators stay calm and controlled—even if the other party gets upset in heated discussions. They master their moods, keep their tone of voice upbeat, maintain a normal volume, and avoid negative body language (such as eye rolls, smirks, or steepled hands). Their less successful colleagues get agitated and react emotionally—only to regret the results later.

(Of course, many negotiations involve complete teams rather than just two people. But since this book focuses on individual leaders, I'm including here only guidelines that apply to individuals. For a more extensive discussion on negotiation strategies and pitfalls, see my book *Communicate With Confidence.*)

Coupled with pre-planning and proper structure, strategic negotiations with lasting benefits for both parties stem from skill and patience—both of which can sometimes be in short supply.

CHAPTER 23

Aim to Do the Second Deal

Don't raise your voice; improve your argument.

—UNKNOWN

Negotiate each situation as if a more important opportunity will rest on the relationship developed in the current interaction.

The failure to operate by this principle underscores why many mergers fall apart at the last minute: One or both parties still lack basic respect and trust of the other because of the way they've been treated throughout the negotiations. The merger breakdown comes down to the "heart of the matter."

For that reason, avoid the term *negotiate* whenever possible. For many people, that word implies a winner and a loser, or at best a compromise between two parties—neither of whom walks away completely satisfied with the outcome. In different circumstances, you might substitute these phrases: "come to an agreement," "work out arrangements," "determine a feasible work plan," "identify a structure that works for all parties," or "set up a workable framework for future projects together." Such phrasing establishes a friendly atmosphere from the get-go.

But in addition to paying attention to phrasing, dig deeper to consider carefully your core negotiation philosophy: Is it to crush the other side? To win at all cost? To do the deal or die? To eke out some kind of arrangement with the other party who trapped you into the deal? That philosophy often shapes your wording. And your wording often drives the outcome.

Your attitude about the negotiation outcome will color the personal relationships with all people involved, the implementation and all further interactions, and the motivation to do future projects together. A strategic communicator understands this.

When you meet great negotiators, you'll recognize the attitude immediately. Two such outstanding negotiators come to mind from my own business.

Gene, formerly a vice president at Shell Oil and at the time CEO of a high-tech software firm, approached me about licensing rights to some of my intellectual property for web-based training programs. During our first two-hour meeting, all his questions focused on "What do *you* need out of this arrangement?" During our more than two-decade partnership (and five product lines developed together), the tenor of the relationship has never changed.

Although our contract has had to be modified through the years as technology and delivery methods have changed, I attribute the successful negotiation to the goal of Gene and the other company owners from the very beginning: mutual benefit. With each change, they approached me with questions: "What works for you?" "Do you want to review and approve each program for quality control?" "What do you think about attending this or that trade show?"

The same could be said of the negotiation with Encyclopaedia Britannica many years ago. Our relationship started when a vice president from their organization attended one of my keynotes. Afterward, the VP extended an invitation to breakfast to meet several other team members and discuss the possibility of licensing the intellectual property. The entire first year of our relationship proved to be all about Britannica having its own clients evaluate my materials: Is this a good fit? Does this work for *you*? What's *your* evaluation of the Booher product line?

Once Britannica received sign-off from their own clients, they moved to negotiate a contract with me. But again, their attitude was "How can we help you grow your business? What's good for you is good for us!" As I wrote other books through the years, they celebrated in a big way—with autograph parties, with introductions to their clients, by including my books in their mailings, by having me autograph books in their trade-show booths. When I voiced new ideas for other products, their response was "Let's do it!"

For more than two decades, until the Britannica Corporate Training division was sold, this relationship proved to be a strategic partnership for both entities—attributable in large part to the spirit of the Britannica negotiators.

The mindset of a strategic negotiator mimics that of a professional salesperson. Just as the salesperson is working to make not a sale but a lifetime customer, the strategic negotiator is trying to negotiate not one deal but a long-term relationship. And even in situations when you're likely negotiating with a party only once, information about your negotiation style and attitude gets around. Word travels throughout your organization and industry. Ask any sales manager, courtroom attorney, or civic leader.

It's all about the *next* opportunity. And the next. And the next. That's why savvy negotiators pay attention to winning the heart (not just the deal) throughout the negotiation process.

PART 4

STRATEGIC SPEAKING
Persuade Minds
and Win Hearts

*Any intelligent fool can make things bigger, more complex,
and more violent. It takes a touch of genius—and a lot of
courage—to move in the opposite direction.*

> —ALBERT EINSTEIN,
> INVENTOR AND PHYSICIST

Facts alone seldom persuade and rarely inspire.

> —BOYD CLARKE AND RON CROSSLAND,
> BUSINESS AUTHORS AND CONSULTANTS

*When you forget yourself and your fear, when you get
beyond self-consciousness because your mind is thinking
about what you are trying to communicate, you become
a better communicator.*

> —PEGGY NOONAN, SPEECHWRITER
> AND SPECIAL ASSISTANT TO
> PRESIDENT RONALD REAGAN

CHAPTER 24

Increase Your Executive Presence

*How you act (gravitas), how you speak
(communication), and how you look (appearance)
count for a lot in determining your leadership presence.*
—SYLVIA ANN HEWLETT,
AUTHOR AND CONSULTANT

Consider personal presence like physical fitness or intelligence. Simply rate yourself somewhere on a continuum from diseased to healthy, unfit to fit, grotesque to attractive, ignorant to genius. There's always room to slide the gauge a notch or two along the scale.

Polling audience after audience, I hear the same 25 to 30 attributes mentioned repeatedly when I ask what skills, traits, attitudes, characteristics, or habits come to mind when they think of executive presence. My book *Creating Personal Presence* divides those attributes into four categories, as shown in the following list.

- **How someone looks:** physical appearance, including body language, dress, accessories, grooming; energy, passion, spirit; surroundings, such as personal work space

- **How someone talks:** speaking patterns and vocal quality; tone of voice that reveals attitude; word choices and use of language; ability to carry on a conversation; emotional reactions and outbursts

- **How someone thinks:** capacity to think strategically, to cut through clutter, to summarize well; ability to organize ideas coherently; ability to think visually and communicate with stories, analogies, metaphors, and sound bites to make messages clear and memorable; ability to think on your feet under pressure

- **How someone acts:** acting consistently with integrity; demonstrating a willingness to listen to others' ideas; engaging with others; being approachable; being genuine; demonstrating thoughtfulness and good manners out of a sense of humility rather than arrogance; having a sense of humor; being competent and accountable for results

All four attributes surface as you speak. The applicability of the first three (look, talk, think) seems obvious. But the way you "act" also affects how an audience perceives you, how an audience responds to you, and whether an audience believes you. Audiences judge your transparency, approachability, humility, competence, and credibility—if not during the formal presentation, then during the Q&A period, or in your interactions before or after the program.

Among my coaching clients, four common difficulties occur repeatedly in communicating with their staff and peers. If the following concerns sound familiar to you, the accompanying tips may help.

LOST IN THE WEEDS

These leaders often confess their inability to summarize key points succinctly. They explain, "I came up through the ranks in our organization, so I'm technical and tend to tell people all I know about a situation." Or "I like to be comprehensive. It's hard to know what information the executive team needs to make a decision." Or "I try to give people options, and there are always pros and cons to everything."

The cure for this problem comes down to this: Consider listening to your voicemails. Do you want three minutes of background first, before the caller gets to the point? Or do you prefer that a caller gives you a one-sentence overview and then goes into the necessary details?

Say it in a sentence or two. If your executive team or clients want more detail, they'll ask.

TALKING *AT* PEOPLE, NOT *WITH* THEM

Some leaders lack an understanding of how to connect with a large group. In conversation, they do well. But give them a crowd, and they crumble. While they know what message they want their audience to walk away with, they have little comprehension of how to deliver that message in a way that motivates individuals in a group.

In short, turn this situation around by changing how you think of a presentation: Consider it a conversation—but with numerous people at once. No matter how many people are in the room, visualize yourself talking to only three, five, or seven people. In fact, select three or five people seated in different sections of the room and carry on the conversation with *just* them. Afterward, you may be surprised to learn that everyone in the group thought you were talking to them, not simply those selected few.

Above all, don't lock your eyes on the entire group and move into "lecture mode." If you do, you'll sound like you're teaching a third-grade class.

> ### Sentences That "Talk At"
> "Attend the full two-day conference if you expect to receive the full benefit."

"I'll overview our policy on charitable contributions and then take questions if time."

"The organization has experienced difficult times. But challenges make people and teams stronger in the end."

Sentences That "Talk With"

"I suggest that you attend the entire two-day conference to get the full benefit."

"Let me overview our policy on charitable contributions and see what questions you have."

"We've come through some difficult times as an organization. But I think these challenges can make us all stronger as a team."

LOOSEY-GOOSEY FOR LAID-BACK

Some leaders mistake the "talk with" principle for sloppy posture and low energy. Their intention is to be informal and approachable. Instead, they come across as unprepared and lacking presence. But as a leader, you need to inspire audience members with passion and enthusiasm about your message and goals. And that aim is not necessarily contradictory with being approachable. The demeanor for such an informal delivery means that you might:

- Interact with people in the audience.

- Encourage questions by your wording and open body language. ("What questions do you have?" *Not:* "Are there questions?")

- Ask for examples or illustrations of your points from audience members.

- Let others recall and summarize your key points rather than doing so yourself.

- Give ownership by asking others to develop and articulate their plans to implement your ideas.

- Make others the heroes of your stories.

- Move around, engaging with audience members. Don't stand rigidly in one spot. (Positioning on the platform is to a presentation what paragraphing is to a document.)

- Keep your energy high. Maintain a strong voice, volume, gestures, and movement.

> Some leaders **mistake** the **"talk with"** principle for sloppy posture and low energy. Their intention is to be informal and approachable. Instead, they come across as **unprepared** and **lacking presence**.

For more detailed information about delivering a speech or presentation in an engaging way, see my earlier book *Speak With Confidence: Powerful Presentations That Inform, Inspire, and Persuade.*

BAFFLED BY TOUGH QUESTIONS FROM STRONG PERSONALITIES

Nothing makes leaders look more capable than handling tough questions with credibility and ease—particularly when making a recommendation to a roomful of executives. Yet, in our surveys of professionals at all levels and in many industries, this skill is what most say they lack. To overcome this challenge of fielding hostile or forced-option questions, prepare ahead of time. Of course, you can't prepare for *the* specific question. But you can prepare psychologically:

- Anticipate potential questions on your topic so that you have prepared responses for sensitive issues.

- Buy a few seconds of thinking time before plunging into an ill-formed answer (pause, look reflective, acknowledge the question, take a sip of water, change positions in the room, ask the person to elaborate on the question, relay the question to someone else for an opinion first).

- Begin with a broad generalization that everyone can agree with, then move forward. (Example: "I know we all want to see these charities thrive and be able to help people in need. Determining the proper contribution can be difficult for many reasons. . . .")

Never let a lack of personal presence stall your career. Every speech serves as a strategic opportunity to showcase both substance and style.

Nothing makes leaders look more capable than **handling tough questions with credibility and ease**.

CHAPTER 25

Dump Your Data to a **Storyline**

*First learn the meaning of
what you say, and then speak.*

— EPICTETUS,
GREEK PHILOSOPHER

In our work culture, leaders rarely just point and tell people where to go and what to do. Instead, they go to a group and make a case. That group may be their own board of directors, their executive team, a client's executive team, a project team, their own staff, or the general public. Even the president sometimes takes a case directly to the voters to drum up support in getting legislation passed.

If you're a marketer, sales professional, engineer, health-care provider, or financial advisor, you'll likely need data on occasion to introduce a new strategy, report, or product, or to take advantage of an unexpected opportunity. Data will help you build your case—but only if you present it in a coherent storyline.

But rather than building a case with a distinctive storyline, some speakers settle for presentation stew. And audiences dislike stew about as much as my teens always did.

"What's wrong with stew?" I asked my daughter.

"I don't like eating food that's all mixed together."

"Well, it'll be mixed all together by the time it gets to your stomach."

"Maybe so. But I still want it separate on the way down."

We never settled the food argument. But I've noticed over the years that audiences don't like presentation stew either. Not a little lump of this and a little lump of that.

Here's how "presentation stew" almost happened at a client site recently. Having listened to the dry run of the client's presentation for the upcoming annual meeting for managers in the field, I'd concluded that the executive team had nothing new to say—it was going to be "business as usual" the following year.

So I asked, "Okay, what's the *new* message you want to get across to your team at this meeting?" The president and four VPs sitting around the conference table stared at each other for a few minutes. Then a couple of them tossed out ideas only to be shot down by a colleague's "No, I don't think *that's* the message we want to deliver."

I waited for agreement. Finally, after listening to his VPs discuss the options for 20 minutes, the president offered a tentative response to my original question. "I think our new message this year is this: 'We met our goal to increase market share by eight percent last year. But we have lots of opportunity to grow market share next year by selling two product lines that we've neglected in the past.' "

"Is that *really* what we want to say?" The VP of Sales spoke up again. "I thought this update was to report specifically how we'd performed in each of our product lines by region."

"Hmmm," the VP of Operations said. "Then why do you have me giving all this information about how we've improved customer service in Region 7?"

Another half hour of discussion followed. After they determined their *real* message and purpose, they realized that nothing in their prepared presentation and slide deck actually delivered that message and built a persuasive case to spur their sales team to sell the two neglected product lines.

I wish this scene were an isolated case. It is not. This "presentation stew" is quite typical.

Consider these tips to tie your data to a storyline to make it clear and memorable.

Determine what story you plan to tell with your facts or data. Then select only the data you need to make your points clear, credible, and memorable. Think like movie scriptwriters. They don't set out to write about every day in the life of a character—or even every day in the romance between John and Jane. They select a few key scenes. Boy meets girl. Boy loses girl. Boy wins the lottery. Boy gets girl. Map out your storyline (or key points) before creating *any* slides or before putting *any* data on a slide.

You can "map out" the story with Post-It notes on your conference room table, with an idea wheel (see my book *Speak With Confidence* for examples), or with a simple list of key topics. This idea is simply to put together the skeleton story first, before developing the details.

Decide which points of your presentation need data support. Like the novelist who knows a lot more about the characters than the novel presents, you typically have much more data than you will ever use. Be selective; use data sparingly—or your audience will remember nothing.

Your goal is to present either an informative briefing or a persuasive case—not necessarily a comprehensive case. Again, consider your storyline. Who's the audience? What's the bottom-line message of interest to that audience? What do they already know? (Don't tell them that!) How will they need to use your information? These questions should guide your storyline and data selection.

Think of words and concepts to convey your conclusion. For example, in my work in the defense industry, I've seen engineers start with 60 slides for a 20-minute briefing. But maybe only eight of those slides illustrate the 12 percent rejection rate because of a faulty widget. Rather than eight charts that show where in the manufacturing process the defects are happening, the engineer really needs only *one* number and *one* chart—or maybe *no* chart at all.

If the engineer intends to focus on the manufacturing step causing the high-reject problem, *one* chart should show that step in the process where 98 percent of the problems occur, coupled with the $XXXX cost, along with the 12 percent rejection rate. That chart would tell the whole story (what problem needs to be corrected and why).

Whether you're developing a speech, preparing for a media interview, meeting with a client, pitching a proposal to your boss, or persuading parents of the soccer team to foot the bill to upgrade the soccer field, focus. Pick *one* point to get across. Then build your storyline by adding supporting data.

Everything flows from the story you're telling.

> Your goal is to present either an **informative briefing** or a **persuasive case—not** necessarily a comprehensive case.

CHAPTER 26

Engage With Great Stories

Those who tell the stories rule society.

—PLATO, GREEK
PHILOSOPHER

Storytelling is no longer considered an "art" mastered by only the few; it has become a fundamental leadership skill, like writing, speaking, and vision-casting. As a communicator, you'll need to select and weave high-impact stories into your presentations, talks, meetings, and conversations to drive home strategic messages and engage others in your cause.

WHY TELL A STORY?

People expect to hear your stories. They've been listening to bedtime stories since birth. If they're Millennials or younger, they've been watching movies on smartphones since they could turn one on. And if coworkers or staff members are old enough to remember walking to school (versus riding), then chances are they've been entertained by great storytellers since they've had access to books, radio, and TV.

Stories involve the listener in the struggle. Listeners (spouse, employees, coworkers, suppliers) begin to identify with the hero in the story, trying to solve the problem and reach the goal. Empathy sets in. As the hero overcomes this and that setback, the listener identifies with *similar* problems—or at least the frustrations and disappointment such problems cause. Bingo. The storyteller has a link to win hearts regarding a similar situation or viewpoint.

Stories forge a deeper involvement and engage emotions on many levels. The details necessary to set the scene and to structure the story involve multiple senses: The physical scene. The appearance of people, things, or places. Hearing—conversations, disturbances, arguments, laughter. The emotional scene: Fear. Starkness. Withdrawal. Shyness. Mockery. Embarrassment. Grief. Love. Forgiveness. Stories create a deeper emotional link to the storyteller's viewpoint, situation, or goal.

Stories bring closure on a significant goal. Similar to how viewers feel at the end of a movie, listeners feel a sense of closure and satisfaction after the story "ends." Whether the movie or story ends "happily ever after" or butts up against a harsh reality, there is still closure—a truth to be processed and internalized.

Stories increase retention. Because stories have structure and the elements of emotion and engagement, they stick in the mind better than straightforward information, concepts, or data. Although good speakers know how to tell an anecdote well, a story stays in the psyche because it has a definite arch that is always the same: beginning, middle, end.

The TED Talks franchise around the world has highlighted the popularity of stories and discussions of "voice." In these 18-minute talks, note that the most-watched speeches—even those on technical topics involving science and mathematics—include stories. Steve Jobs told stories to launch his Apple products successfully. Warren Buffett tells stories about his investment strategies and philosophies. Creativity expert Ken Robinson, the most popular TED Talks speaker of all time, tells stories about failures in our educational system. World leaders tell stories about what they've achieved and where they want to take the country in the future. And the stories usually include aspects of vulnerability and failure.

Publications such as *Harvard Business Review*, *Forbes*, *The Wall Street Journal*, *INC*, *Fast Company*, *Success*, and *Entrepreneur* routinely ask CEOs for their stories: How did you get started? When have you failed and what did that experience teach you? How has your upbringing prepared you for life and your current career? If you could have a do-over, what would that be and why? What have you learned about leadership and how did you learn that?

So if you're convinced that stories are fundamental to speaking as a strategic leader, why do some storytellers elicit little more than a blank stare?

1. Mistaking an anecdote for a story

2. Inappropriate story *structure*

3. Failure to *deliver* the story with impact

Let's take these issues one at a time.

> *Storytelling* is no longer considered an "art" mastered by only the few; it has become a *fundamental leadership skill*, like writing, speaking, and vision-casting.

ANECDOTES VERSUS STORIES

An anecdote can simply be an incident, a happening, or a "slice of life." It may be sad, funny, tragic, odd, or merely amusing. Examples: Telling how badly a customer service rep treated you. Explaining the terrible ski accident your spouse had last vacation. Relating your boss's first experience of being fired and how that motivated her to start her own company.

A story, by contrast, has an official literary definition that you may recall from English class: A hero or heroine struggles to overcome obstacles to reach an important goal. The hero may be the storyteller, another person like your Uncle Frank or your next-door neighbor, or a group. (Other examples: The "hero" might be an organization struggling to stay afloat and avoid bankruptcy. Or the "hero" might even be an inanimate object—like a new product developed on a shoestring budget struggling to become number one in the marketplace. Or the "hero" might be a team struggling to prove its worth and avoid being downsized during a merger.)

Obstacles that get in the way of reaching the important goal might be a disapproving boss, a tight budget, lack of experience, stupidity, a forced relocation, a death in the family, a senseless internal company policy, or bad weather. You get the picture.

An important goal might be physical safety, a successful product launch, good health, a proper sense of self, profitability, integrity, saving your company, "doing the right thing," stronger self-confidence, mastery of a new skill, or any number of things the "hero" hopes to achieve by the end of the struggle.

Structure a good storyline, and listeners will root for the hero all the way to the end!

APPROPRIATE STORY STRUCTURE

No one watching a TV documentary would mistake it for an action thriller or a romance movie. Sure, they all involve video footage of people. But that's where the similarities end. Documentaries have a typical structure. Action movies have a typical structure. Romance movies have a typical structure. Documentaries make a point—but they don't "tell a story" in the same sense that a mystery or romance does.

The typical story follows a basic structure.

If you've lived, you have superb stories. Becoming a skillful storyteller involves paying attention—recognizing those situations, events, and occurrences that make first-rate stories and then shaping those stories to share valuable insights.

SKELETON
STORY STRUCTURE

Hero (all is well)

↓

Problem Develops or Disruption Happens

↓

Goal Forms (hero now has an important goal to reach—one the audience cares about)

↓

Obstacle (complicates the hero's attempt to reach the goal)

↓

Another Obstacle (further problem / delay complicating the hero's journey to reach the goal)

↓

Another Obstacle (further problem / delay complicating the hero's journey to reach the goal)

↓

Hero Finally Achieves Goal (all is well again)

Note: You can toss in as many obstacles as appropriate—or as authentic or as time permits—to build the story.

Polish your storytelling with a solid story skeleton.

Unless you're a walking memory bank (most of us aren't), you'll need to record these stories as they occur to you. That doesn't mean you'll instantly recognize how you can best use the story to make a significant point in an upcoming speech, presentation, meeting, party, or conversation. But when something odd, humorous, or meaningful happens, note it—either write it down or record it on your smartphone and email it to yourself. Then title the file in a way you'll remember the incident. Save your stories in a "Stories" folder or journal. (Ministers, rabbis, priests, professors, consultants, and professional speakers do this routinely.)

Then when the next occasion presents itself to speak, browse through your file and select your supporting stories to make your key points.

DELIVER THE STORY WITH IMPACT

The final reason stories land with a thud: weak delivery. No matter how great the story, you can kill it in the telling with little or no thought on how to set it up, shape it, phrase it, and land it. See the checklist for help.

The next time you need to inspire your team, launch a new initiative, or motivate people to accomplish a mission, perfect this storytelling art: Select a *real* story, shape it into the proper structure, and deliver it well. In strategic situations, a great story can make the difference between inspiration and a blank stare.

> No matter how great **the story,** you can kill it in the telling with little or no thought **on how to set it up, shape it, phrase it, and land it**.

CHECKLIST FOR A
DYNAMIC DELIVERY

- Set up your story in an intriguing way. Use an opening line that makes people say, "Tell me more" or "What do you mean by that?" (Example: "Whoever said absence makes the heart grow fonder hasn't lived next door to Bubbles McGuire.")

- Introduce the hero in a colorful manner. (Is there something odd about this person to help listeners immediately visualize and understand him or her?)

- Include details. Help the audience visualize the scene.

- Eliminate superfluous details that slow the action and add nothing but length.

- Add dialogue. Don't tell us what the characters said. Bring in the characters and let us hear them talk, argue, pout, ignore, misunderstand, or shout.

- Use colorful phrasing. Replace vague words with specifics. Not "car" but "2012 Chevy pickup." Not "reading a magazine" but "reading a Delta *Sky Magazine* with only the shopping pages left."

- End with the punch line, putting the punch word at the end. (Even serious stories have a punch line—a poignant ending.)

- Let the story stand on its own. Don't explain it. If people don't get the point, either you need to rework the story or you need a better story.

- Transition to your key point for the story. What insights did you gain from this event or situation? What's the takeaway for your listeners? What insights did you or the hero gain through the struggle, failure, success, journey, or outcome?

Great stories die for lack of a dynamic delivery.

CHAPTER 27

Be Brief or Be Dismissed

Make sure you have finished speaking
before your audience has finished listening.

—DOROTHY SARNOFF,
OPERA SINGER, ACTRESS,
AND SELF-HELP PIONEER

Have you ever watched a TV broadcast live during an emergency situation—weather, crime, terrorist attack? Notice that the TV anchor continues to restate the same few facts available.

"You're watching a live scene now from Atlanta, Georgia. We're waiting to hear a word from the president any moment. We'll bring you more details as we have them. . . . Chaos unfolds all around us. The president will be joining us shortly in a press conference. In case you've just joined us, we're watching a scene live now from Atlanta, where the president will be touching down shortly in Air Force One. That should be any moment now. This scene is remarkable. Difficult to tell what's happening. If you've just tuned in, you're watching a scene now live from Atlanta. . . ."

On and on and on, the anchor repeats, trying to hold viewers while the cameras roll. After a few minutes of this, impatient viewers start to flip channels. Fewer and fewer people are inclined to let others waste their time—particularly to listen to something they could read in one-sixth the time on a website or social media.

Brevity gives focus. And with focus comes clarity.

Consider these five best practices to make the most of situations when you speak.

As an "off-the-cuff" speaker, avoid spontaneous rambles. If you're nominated for an award, think positively and plan what you'll say if you win. Conventional thinking leads speakers to believe that their off-the-cuff comments will be brief because they're unscripted. The opposite most often proves true. Spontaneous speakers sound like that TV anchor trying to hold viewers. When speakers are called on to "say a few words" without having given their comments any forethought, they often ramble until they figure out what they want to say. Don't. Pause. Think. Say it and be seated.

As a presenter, organize business presentations in the decision maker's format. That is, begin with a summary. Make your bottom line your opening line. Tell the audience what you want them to do, decide, approve, consider, buy, or learn as you elaborate further. You may be shocked at how many details become unnecessary after a succinct summary up front. Our consultants have taught this format to business audiences in many countries and cultures, and executives have yet to tell us they disapprove. The summary-first structure provides context for the details that follow.

As a keynoter, edit a prepared speech script ruthlessly. Think thin. Rehearse. Time each key point so that you can adjust timing on the fly if necessary. Although I suggest that you learn your content and speak from a key-word outline rather than a full script, a full script may be appropriate at times. (If so, ten minutes invested in editing will improve clarity and strengthen the message.)

As a meeting participant, prepare your contributions. Review the agenda beforehand, and prepare your comments so you can deliver them concisely. Keep details and data at hand so your comments don't devolve into a ramble.

As emcee or facilitator, eliminate the lag time in your events. Consider your sales meetings, management meetings, or other conferences scheduled over two to four days. How much time is devoted to announcements, logistics, an agenda overview—in general, telling people what they've already read in the program? If you're the emcee, cut these redundancies.

Television viewers who regularly record favorite programs know they can watch the DVR version in about half the time it takes to watch the live version by simply fast-forwarding through commercials. Consider analyzing the productive parts of your meetings versus the "downtimes": late starts, off-topic discussions, delays waiting for missing information, and so forth. Eliminate such time wasters so that the one-hour meeting can be reduced to a half hour. If you're in charge, lead. If the meeting runs overtime, the group will blame you as the emcee, facilitator, or leader. (More about running efficient meetings in a later section of this book.)

> **Brevity** gives focus. And with **focus** comes clarity.

According to Shakespeare, "Brevity is the soul of wit." In today's workplace, brevity is a key to the executive suite.

CHAPTER 28

Prepare for Off-the-Cuff Comments

The words a leader speaks are important, of course.
But how they're delivered can make all the difference.
Especially in tough times.

—JOHN BALDONI,
LEADERSHIP AUTHOR
AND COACH

I f you're a leader, you'll be called on from time to time to "say a few words." The occasions vary: Kicking off a conference or meeting. Commemorating an anniversary. Celebrating a holiday. Congratulating your coworkers or staff on a job well done. Answering a relayed question from your boss before a larger group. Receiving or presenting an award.

Ideally, someone will notify you of such events ahead of time so you can prepare. Rest assured that many people who seem to be speaking extemporaneously are not. They've prepared to be "spontaneous."

That is, they've learned a few "evergreen" comments for such occasions that they can tailor on the spot. Mark Twain is often quoted as saying, "It usually takes me more than three weeks to prepare a good impromptu speech."

But even if you don't receive notice to prepare the exact content, you can follow a ready-made *structure* that will help you think on your feet in high-pressure moments. I suggest The LEAD Format™ for extemporaneous comments.

Using this format for an award presentation, a celebration, a commendation, a kick-off event, or emceeing works. Your content doesn't have to be all that creative. The structure works particularly well for giving opinions or answering questions. The format provides great flexibility—you can use it for a 15-second off-the-cuff comment or a 5-minute response to a question.

In either case, long or short, the structure guides your thinking and keeps your comments coherent. Don't get stuck in ramble mode, circling and circling and circling, looking for a place to land. Instead, remember The LEAD Format™ for those high-pressure, high-visibility, strategic opportunities to show how well you think on your feet.

Don't get stuck
in ramble mode,
circling and circling and circling,
                    looking for a place
                              to land.

THE LEAD FORMAT™ FOR SPEAKING EXTEMPORANEOUSLY AND THINKING ON YOUR FEET

	Defined	Examples
Lead	(*noun, as in newspaper lead*) Summarize in a sentence or two what you think or feel about the situation, occasion, event, award, or accomplishment.	• "I'm thrilled to present this award because I know the struggle that went into winning it." • "This has to be the second most exciting evening of my life—surpassed only by dragging my beloved down the wedding aisle." • "Today represents a somber occasion as we mark the first anniversary of the tragedy of X." • "Panels like this confuse me. Are these panelists on the stage real or ninjas? Their credentials are mind-boggling!"
Elaboration	Elaborate on your opening statement. Give reasons or explanation.	"This award involves hard work... Second, this award represents... Third, the winner of this award must..."
Anecdote	Tell an anecdote to illustrate your point.	A brief anecdote will engage your listeners emotionally and further illustrate your key point, reasons, or explanations.
Digest	End with the *Reader's Digest Condensed* version of your opening statement.	"So, let me wrap up by saying that I'm thrilled to present the XX award for service and excellence to Joe Schmoe."

Use The LEAD Format™ for thinking on your feet to speak extemporaneously.

THE LEAD FORMAT™: AN EXAMPLE

Lead	Thank you for taking the time to stop by this afternoon to help us celebrate winning the $227 million Kruxton contract—our first in the health-care industry.
Elaboration	These three people standing before you—Juan Castillo, Jennifer Dyer, and Peter Taka—won it after more than eight hard-fought months of meetings, proposals, and paperwork. Their effort involved a three-volume proposal (more than 2,000 pages). They spent several long weekends traveling to Stockholm and back for meetings. And they slogged through countless hours of federal regulations and legal opinions to make sure they dotted all the *i*'s and crossed all the *t*'s. Not to mention getting grilled by our own legal team!
Anecdote	Let me give you just one window into this effort: You know how cumbersome travel has become. On one of these "quick" trips to Sweden, it was definitely planned and coordinated by Murphy, with Murphy's Law definitely in play. Juan, Jennifer, and Peter's flight sat on the runway for four hours before taking off. Then they had an emergency landing, I think in LA, to refuel before they ever left the States. Then they landed in Stockholm with temperatures well below zero. Only to discover that their luggage had not arrived. They had to wear the same clothes both days while there negotiating. Yes, they looked very authoritative in jeans! Returned home before their luggage was ever found. Then got detained at our border because they were traveling internationally with no luggage! And these mishaps were all part of just *one* trip. Needless to say, this contract did not involve those ideal fringe travel benefits and three-martini lunches taxpayers keep talking about!
Digest	So definitely, this coup took stamina and determination, along with expertise. Please join me in giving Juan, Jennifer, and Peter a big round of applause to celebrate the $227 million Kruxton contract—a huge win for our company.

Plan impromptu comments with The LEAD Format™ so you can think on your feet under pressure—such as when called on to "say a few words."

PART 5

STRATEGIC WRITING

Write to the Point

*Writing comes more easily if
you have something to say.*

> —SHOLEM ASCH, NOVELIST
> AND DRAMATIST

People who think well, write well.

> —DAVID OGILVY, BUSINESSMAN,
> KNOWN AS THE "FATHER OF ADVERTISING"
> AND FOUNDER OF ONE OF THE LARGEST
> ADVERTISING AGENCIES IN THE WORLD

Clarity in business writing is not a luxury.

> —SIR RICHARD BRANSON,
> CEO AND ENTREPRENEUR

CHAPTER 29

Let
Them See
How You
Think

If you can't explain it simply,
you don't understand it well enough.

—ALBERT EINSTEIN, INVENTOR
AND PHYSICIST, DEVELOPER OF
THE THEORY OF RELATIVITY

Writing can be a tough task master. Unlike in a meeting or hallway discussion, you can't mumble through the process. Writing demands research, analysis, creativity, and organization. Writing forces you to think—that is, unless you plan to write drivel. And most of us recognize drivel when we see it. Also, unlike spoken words that gradually fade in everyone's memory, a document may last forever in the files.

As you write strategic documents for executive readers, consider these six mind games.

IMAGINE YOURSELF SEEKING CAPITAL FROM
A ROOMFUL OF VENTURE CAPITALISTS

Gaining acceptance for the recommendation you're proposing is rarely a slam dunk. If you feel passionate about the idea, it may be difficult to see downsides or dangers that could derail your success. But eventually, you'll need to roll out enough details so that you or others can implement the idea, project, process, product, or service. Imagine yourself in a conference room surrounded by VCs. What questions will they ask you before investing? Fill in the missing gaps to give a clear, complete, accurate picture.

SIT FOR A FINAL EXAM WITH
YOUR VIRTUAL "BOARD"

To complete a master's degree or PhD program, students face a group of professors while being grilled about everything they've read during the previous two to four years of their study program. Most students report that the experience is grueling. The questions force them to consider all their past reading and to analyze all the divergent ideas, compare and contrast them, summarize them, and apply them in new ways to current situations.

To improve your thinking on your new idea, simulate that experience. Invite three colleagues to get on a conference call with you. Give them a three-minute briefing on your idea (as applicable, include the what, why, when, how, who, and how much).

Then open the floor ten minutes for questions from your colleagues. What else do they need to know before "approving," "sponsoring," "implementing," or "recommending" the idea to others? Don't actually *answer* their questions; just record them. This board exercise will demonstrate what you may have missed in your own first analysis of the idea: Did you leave out important information? Did they connect the proverbial dots in the overview you communicated to them? Did they get sidetracked by nonessential information and miss your key points?

Complete this virtual exercise; then write your document to address their questions and issues. Granted, analytical thinking is hard work, but facing a virtual "board of buddies" can be far less brutal than trying to implement a half-baked idea, project, or policy.

WAIT FOR THE STARTING
GUN TO DRAFT

After you discover what information needs to be included, what questions need to be answered, what objections or concerns need to be addressed, you *still* may not be ready to draft.

In sports, athletes get penalized for false starts. Writers also sometimes start too early. I admire people who "get a jump" on tasks and settle down to a project before a deadline looms. But writing involves more than putting words on the screen or paper. In fact, the toughest part of writing is thinking. When your thinking has been insufficient, and you draft too early, what often drips from your fingertips is drivel.

AVOID THE "SO WHAT?"
GRIMACE

Whether you're writing an email, a proposal, or a report, the document should never leave the reader thinking, "So what? Why did you tell me this? What do you want me to do?" The next action should be clear. Even the most popular social media posts include a call-to-action: "Look at this video." "Listen to this interview." "Read this article." "Take this quiz." "Visit my website." "Attend my webinar." Make sure your document answers the reader's "So what?"

THINK LEAN

Some writers tend to include everything related to the subject that anyone on their distribution list might need or want to know in this lifetime. In doing so, they bury key ideas under the rubble, and primary readers become irritated at the "irrelevant" hodge-podge.

Never do a brain dump. Instead, organize your information for the most important readers. Then for secondary readers (for example, readers on your "cc" list), you have four options:

- Layer the less important information in the detail section of the document under appropriate headings for easy skimming.

- Include the less important details in an attachment.

- Put supplemental details in footnotes or endnotes.

- Provide a source or link to additional information.

Again, your document should not reflect everything you know about a subject. It should reflect everything you think significant to make a decision or take action.

BE "OTHER-FOCUSED," NOT SELF-CONSCIOUS

Consider the following excerpt from the marketing department of a client organization:

> Our department is currently preparing our pre-launch campaign for our route drivers and will be bringing them into headquarters during the next two weeks to give them a preview of our next year's marketing plans. In doing so, we noticed that we do not have collateral materials and pricing on your division's product lines. We need those from you within the next five days so that . . .

Do you notice that everything in this statement is focused on the writer's needs? *OUR department. OUR pre-launch campaign. OUR route drivers. OUR next year's marketing plans. WE noticed that WE do not have . . . WE need those.* Frankly, readers don't care about you, the writer. They care about themselves and what THEY want and need.

Revolutionize the response to your writing by analyzing and focusing on what's of interest to your readers rather than yourself. For example, here's a redo of the previous appeal:

Don't be left out of the pre-launch marketing campaign when the route drivers visit headquarters during the next two weeks. Get your marketing collateral materials and pricing on all your product lines to us within the next five days to ensure that your division will be included in the lineup. Our route drivers will be hearing a preview of next year's marketing plans, including plans on your unit's product lines!

See the strategic difference in the appeal between these two versions?

> Your document **should not** reflect everything you **know** about a subject. It **should** reflect everything you think **significant**.

Having information available tempts productive people to pump out words quickly. As the workplace presents fewer and fewer occasions to talk face to face and on the phone, your texts, emails, posts, and reports reflect—and document forever—your thinking. It pays to think strategically on paper or online.

CHAPTER 30

Trust the TA-DA Template™

When something can be read without effort,
great effort has gone into its writing.

—ENRIQUE JARDIEL PONCELA,
SPANISH PLAYWRIGHT
AND NOVELIST

When an email, report, or proposal confuses people, typically the problem is structure, not content. To translate this concept to digital language: The writer selects the image, edits it, crops it, and *then* decides where he wants to post it. Wrong approach.

A backward display of information leads to either rereading or total incomprehension. Yet people routinely write as they think. They start with "once-upon-a-time-there-was-this-problem" and go all the way through the details of the situation and the investigation finally to "here's-my-summary-of-the-situation-and-solution-THE-END."

The difficulty with this display of information: People can't follow your discussion of the problem and details until they understand your overall point. See what I mean with this example.

Don,

As you know, for the last 5 months, we've been formally evaluating the Call Center to find alternatives to enable our company to reach a certain set of business goals. A few of those goals are to: *(I know this!)*

- Put infrastructure in place to grow in a "campus-like" environment

- Improve response times internally and externally

- Stop giving support away free due to inability to track maintenance agreements

- Reduce extraordinary hold times

(I already knew these goals!)

Our sense of urgency was increased when the company discovered, through a report, that the abandonment rate of calls was extraordinarily high—from 24% to in excess of 50% of customers or potential customers hanging up before making contact.   *(Whoa! That's bad. What are you going to do about it?)*

What we think NetComm offers to us can best be described as business impact, technology, and financial investment. The investment is roughly $2 mil, which can be financed over 3 years. Let me know your thoughts and if you'd like me to set up a meeting with them to answer your questions.

DeAnn

Besides having to read all the way to the end of the document to find out the key message, this email raises more questions than it answers: What "report" revealed the abandonment rate? What is meant by "business impact" and "technology"? Is NetComm making part of the $2 million investment? What's the time frame before this situation is resolved?

Solution: Use the TA-DA Template™ to organize your routine documents (emails, letters, reports, and proposals) in an easy-to-understand format so readers can grasp your point quickly in one reading and take action. Don't leave them wondering, "Now what am I supposed to do?" "Why is this important?" "So what is the cost again?"

THE TA-DA TEMPLATE™ FOR WRITING

T	A	–	D	A
Top-Line Summary	**Action**		**Details**	**Attachments**
	(follow-up or recommendation)		(why, how, where, when, who, how much)	

Trust The TA-DA Template™ for organizing your emails, reports, and proposals in an easy-to-understand format that helps readers grasp your message quickly in one reading.

Don't keep your readers blindfolded halfway through your documents before stating your key message. Putting the message up front will reduce both reader time and tension.

Of course, exceptionally sensitive situations—such as "bad news" messages—warrant a different structure. Start with a neutral or positive opening, add an explanation about the situation or reasons for the "news" you're about to deliver, and then state your negative message. (For a few other exceptions, see *E-Writing: 21st-Century Tools for Effective Communication.*) But for the vast majority of emails, reports, and proposals, the above template will be all you need to be clear, concise, and persuasive.

TA-DA—that performance will generate applause!

Here's the TA-DA Template™ at work, a revision of the previous email.

> Don,
>
> After 5 months of evaluation, we think NetComm is the best business partner to help us improve our Call Center service. Their current study and report has already had significant business impact by revealing that 24–50% of our prospects and customers abandon the call before ever making contact with our Call Center. Additionally, NetComm's specific technology (both software, processes, and staff expertise) complements our environment well to achieve the key business goals we've established for the next 12 months.
>
> Their proposal involves our investment of roughly $2 mil, which can be financed over 3 years.
>
> I plan to meet with them to review the proposal in more detail. If you'd like to attend, please let me know when you're available, and I'll coordinate accordingly.
>
> Just as a reminder, here are a few of the business goals we're working toward:
>
> - Put infrastructure in place to grow in a "campus-like" environment
>
> - Improve response times internally and externally
>
> - Stop giving support away free due to inability to track maintenance agreements
>
> - Reduce extraordinary hold times
>
> I've attached their full proposal if you care to review it.
>
> DeAnn

CHAPTER 31

Use Social Media Strategically—Don't Spray Paint

It's [social media] a highly deceptive world,
one that constantly asks you to comment but
doesn't really care what you have to say.

—DAVID LEVITHAN, AUTHOR

Every morning, a vast majority of people pop awake with the thought "I need to post." Not I need to eat, call home, pray—but post. The second thought is, Post what? What words of wisdom do I have today? If you come up short, then you hope your wise friends have already written a spectacular post that you can "share." If your friends have been slacking off, you have to go hunt for something intriguing at an official publication site and actually read and evaluate its merit before you share it.

Then, of course, there are the related tasks: reading or writing blogs, reading the day's ezines in your inbox, catching up with what's trending on Twitter, retweeting friends' tweets, circling over to LinkedIn to check messages and group discussions, acknowledging all the "Likes" and comments with appropriate responses, sharing a fascinating article from Huffpo, *HBR*, or *Forbes* with a witty lead-in on GooglePlus, then checking Facebook or InstaGram to see who said what about whom. Then there's Pinterest for keeping up with pins from competitor products and services. Then on to YouTube to search for the latest videos on your topic and competitor activities.

Do you really have this kind of time? Of course not! Posting affects productivity. Spending an hour a day on social media amounts to nine weeks a year! Nine weeks! That's enough to complete a couple of college courses toward an advanced degree. Think what you could learn, create, build, give, or master with that time. But probably in the same breath, you'll argue that if you disappear from this scene for a couple of weeks, people will start emailing to ask if you've died or if your organization has gone out of business.

Do you really have this kind of money? Maybe. Maybe not. All the social media sites started out free to users. Now that users have been enticed and hooked, the sites are all being monetized with ads or upgraded plans for users. In addition to paying for advertising and subscribing, many individuals and businesses now hire marketing teams to "participate" for them online.

Do you really have a message that stands out? Maybe. Maybe not. Social media has become white noise. Individuals and small businesses used to say that the internet and social media leveled the playing field—they could occasionally toss in a mention about their product or service on their personal pages or blog and no one would mind. But now everyone uses social media for marketing. Every day, your followers get spray painted with offers about free webinars, free teleseminars, free training, free conferences, free podcasts, free reports, free white papers, and free downloadable ebooks.

People beg you to take their giveaways. Thinking creatively in all the social media noise is like writing your dissertation in the middle of a superhighway. You may get the stimulation of new ideas, but finding space to execute them becomes another matter.

Don't get me wrong: I'm a social person and relatively active on social media. It's just that social media is fast evolving into a cacophony that drowns out authentic communication and drains productivity.

Are you sure people are really "there"? Maybe. Maybe not. Do you really have 379,000 "followers" on Twitter who respond when you suggest they take action? Do you really have 9,273 close "connections" on LinkedIn who would take your call? How many of your 23,267 "friends" on Facebook would recognize your name if they saw it on a billboard?

How do you use social media strategically so that it works FOR rather than AGAINST you? Of course, you could use social media for *great* purposes, as digital analyst Brian Solis has imagined its effect on the world: "Social media spark a revelation that we, the people, have a voice, and through the democratization of content and ideas we can once again unite around common passions, inspire movements, and ignite change."

My assumption: You're going to keep using social media personally and in your business. My recommendation: Use social media *strategically* to accomplish your specific communication goals rather than spray paint your posts everywhere, seeing what sticks where.

> Thinking creatively in all the **social media noise** is like writing your dissertation in the middle of a superhighway.

SELECT THE RIGHT CHANNELS

Social media experts recommend that you choose one or at most two social media platforms. Decide where your ideal customers and colleagues congregate and go there. Study the analytics for that forum—by gender, age, industry, topic, geography, and buying habits.

Learn to use that platform so you're not struggling with the features you frequently need. If you're going to engage on any platform, learn to play there productively. Either dig around on the platform yourself, get a neighborhood teenager to tutor you, take an online course, search how-to videos on YouTube, or learn from a younger staff member. (Going the "younger staff member" route often leads to a mutually beneficial, two-way mentoring relationship.)

LIMIT YOUR SESSION

Social media can be addictive. If you don't believe it, notice how many minutes (or hours) you can spend on your favorite platform on a rainy Saturday afternoon when you have no family or leisure activities planned. Before you know it, your fifteen minutes has turned into five hours.

Decide how much time you can devote to social media (personal, social, or business), blogging, posting product or service offers, checking on competitive activities, making product offers, reading industry news, responding to questions in chat groups, sharing educational tips, encouraging referrals from your customers, posting case studies, introducing new product or service launches, running contests or discounts, posting routine status updates, posting thought-provoking questions, sharing your expert opinion on industry forums, and so forth. Select those that work for your business and your audience.

Then set an alarm. When time's up, stop for the day.

DELIVER A CONSISTENT MESSAGE

As with branding on products or services, when you post, stay on topic. Yes, social media experts recommend that you let your personality shine through and post items of a personal (versus business) nature every so often at a ratio of about 10:1 (business to personal).

But in business messages, keep a consistent theme. If your firm offers legal services, you'll get little return on posts supplying recipes or DIY home makeovers. And off-topic posts will likely confuse your followers. (Yes, such posts may get many "Likes," but they will not necessarily get you closer to your goal of conversion.)

Your blogs, tweets, Facebook posts, YouTube videos, or Pinterest boards should not bewilder people about your overall brand and the message you want to convey—especially if your posts represent your organization. If your visitors don't understand your value, your message, or your mission, then they'll likely not continue the relationship.

ENGAGE PEOPLE—DON'T GET SIDETRACKED BY THE NUMBERS

Keep in mind that it's more important to have real conversations with real people than to have a large number of followers. Post or tweet things of value. If someone comments on a post, respond sensibly. Ask questions. Listen for input. As nearly as possible, communicate with people online as you would at a get-together of your colleagues.

Then when you need to ask for help, people will respond in kind with action. And who doesn't need help from their friends from time to time? Help with referrals and recommendations. With opinions. With answers. With resources. With leads. With sales.

DRIVE THE TRAFFIC TO YOUR OWN SITE

Consider social media like leased office space. Your landlord may permit you to add built-in shelving in the breakroom as long as you cover the expense yourself. But if the building owner decides to sell the building and tells you to find new office space, the new shelving will remain with the building. You'll discover that your $18,000 investment to remodel is gone.

Unless the bulk of your traffic comes to your own blog, you're in a similar situation. Building a following on social media comes with this caveat: The rules of engagement may change at any time. Because you're building your following on rental property, proceed with caution.

Solution: Make it your ultimate goal to use your social media channels to drive traffic to your own website. There you're a property owner, not a renter. As the domain owner, you can control the communication and the traffic.

Keep in mind that it's more important to **have real conversations** with **real people** than to have a large number of followers.

With forethought, social media posts *can* be strategic in reaching your goals. Just be sure you know what your goals are! Without a strategic plan, communicating on social media is about as predictable and significant as spray paint on a very windy day.

PART 6

STRATEGIC MEETINGS

Deliver Results
When You Meet

*The quality of business communications has become
poorer in recent years as people avoid phone calls and
face-to-face meetings, I can only assume, in some
misguided quest for efficiency.*

—SIR RICHARD BRANSON,
CEO AND ENTREPRENEUR

*The ability to express an idea is well
nigh as important as the idea itself.*

—BERNARD BARUCH, FINANCIER,
INVESTOR, AND PHILANTHROPIST

*Meetings . . . are rather like cocktail parties.
You don't want to go but you're cross not to be asked.*

—JILLY COOPER,
JOURNALIST AND AUTHOR

CHAPTER 32

Consider a **Meeting** **Before** the Meeting

Before you state your case,
gather the evidence, especially
what motivates the other person.

—DENIS WAITLEY,
MOTIVATIONAL SPEAKER
AND AUTHOR

While developing a proposal writing program for a client, I brought up the importance of understanding the specs in client RFPs—especially when those requests for proposals contained ambiguities. I had ready examples of ambiguously phrased requirements from the client RFPs to prove my point.

The marketing director looked at me with surprise: "Oh, we'd be in *big* trouble if we had to understand those poorly drafted RFPs! Hopefully, we've met with a customer's liaison *long* before this stage and helped shape that RFP before it comes to us formally."

A real eye-opener early in my consulting career—and a key strategy for sales professionals. Since those early years, I've observed and learned from other leaders to apply the strategy much more broadly:

- To gather individual input about team issues in the future (aspirations, fears, potential obstacles, desired assignments)—things that team members might be hesitant to mention in a group but will gladly share with you one on one

- To do a "commitment check" before an official vote (to gain an understanding of the degree of passion individuals feel about a certain project or policy)

- To solicit support for a recommendation to be presented at a later meeting

- To ask for input about "potential obstacles" on an idea before presenting it in a larger meeting

- To solicit "champions" to help resolve ongoing problems in group dynamics of the meetings

- To verify facts and procedures before a meeting when the leader anticipates disruption

- To interview coworkers and staff to discern personal hidden agendas before discussing a controversial issue in an open forum

- To develop a criteria matrix for a decision that will need to be made in a larger, later meeting

- To discuss with key stakeholders who have either veto power or budget approval *their* criteria for a decision that will need to be made in a larger, later meeting

- To confirm primary goals and non-negotiables with all parties before mediating a conflict and trying to bring two parties to resolution

Before a rock-star performer comes on stage, a warm-up act loosens up the crowd to enjoy the concert. Similarly, you may need to coordinate a warm-up act before your strategic meeting.

CHAPTER 33

Plug Power Into Your Agenda

It isn't that they can't see the solution.
It is that they can't see the problem.

—G. K. CHESTERTON, 20TH-CENTURY
ENGLISH WRITER, PHILOSOPHER,
AND THEOLOGIAN

L et's start with the idea that you need an agenda—and not simply the topics in the meeting leader's head. For those who use an agenda regularly, great. Next step: Make it functional.

The typical agenda for business meetings sounds as appealing to attendees as a bottle of lukewarm water to sunbathers on a hot summer day at the beach. While the topics listed may be routine, they're rarely functional, engaging, or energizing. For example, a typical agenda for a staff meeting might look like this:

Weekly Status Updates

Headquarters News

Product Updates

Cost Reductions

Head Count

Vacations/Absences

Regional Visit July 14

For a client meeting, the routine agenda rarely looks more rousing:

Introductions of the Team

Capabilities Overview

Project Objectives

Discussion of Research/
Interviews

Budget/Pricing

Questions?

> **Why** do topic agendas **not** work as well as they should? They're **too broad to inform** and **too difficult to control**.

Why do such agendas not work as well as they should? They're too broad to inform and too difficult to control. For meetings to be productive, discussions need to be laser-focused on the issues at hand.

Solution: Shape your agenda "topics" into questions. The above weekly staff meeting agenda looks different in a question format.

With this sharply focused agenda, all participants immediately know the exact points of the discussion—the input needed, the problem to be solved, or the decision to be made. Hitting the target is far easier when everyone knows the intended outcome.

> A **strategically structured** agenda is to a meeting what a foundation is to a **skyscraper**.

As meeting leader, you drive the discussion by the questions you ask. A strategically structured agenda is to a meeting what a foundation is to a skyscraper. With this functional document, you can build significant analysis and discussions that lead to solid decisions and action.

SAMPLE AGENDA
IN QUESTION FORMAT

Topics	Questions on Issues or Updates
Weekly Status Updates	—What progress did you make on your top two accounts this week? —Have there been any unexpected delays in closing dates already reported?
Headquarters News	—What "merger scuttlebutt" have you heard from suppliers, competitors, clients, or prospects?
Product Updates	—What is the best/simplest explanation to give customers regarding our delayed launch of Model 450?
Cost Reductions	—Where can you cut cost by 5 percent in your area? —How can we best gather cost-reduction ideas from all employees in our division?
Head Count	—Can you provide an accurate head count by category by the end of the week? (If not, I'll need to delay the RG report.)
Vacations/Absences	—Will we have problems with coverage during summer months? —Should we reconsider the one-week shutdown policy next year?
Regional Visit July 14	—Are your people prepared for the physical audit of the plant? If not, what immediate actions need to be taken?

Prepare your agendas in question format to focus your discussion.

CHAPTER 34

Make Little Meeting Matters a Big Deal

*Effective meetings don't happen
by accident; they happen by design.*

—UNKNOWN

As with race cars, what's "under the hood" drives a meeting's over-all success. Don't be misled by the phrase "meeting details," as in "Someone will get back to you with the meeting details."

A key reason for so many nonproductive meetings is meeting leaders' failure to understand the strategy behind the "details." As a result, those same leaders turn the decisions about the "details" over to their administrative support staff. Big mistake!

Support staff can coordinate the meeting and *implement* the "details," of course. But you as meeting leader need to make the strategic decisions that often determine what happens in the meeting. If your meeting creates frustration and accomplishes nothing, attendees will blame you, the leader—not the admin staff.

Consider the typical time wasters in those meetings *you* dread to attend and determine not to let these be said of your meetings:

- Meeting called at the last minute so people come unprepared

- Meeting canceled at the last minute (disrupted schedules)

- Meeting not canceled but should have been because key people failed to attend (must meet again)

- Late arrivers (have to recap for them)

- Early leavers (decisions postponed because key people leave early)

- Attendees know of meeting but didn't bring appropriate information

- Group too large to have meaningful discussion

- Group too small to have fresh ideas or perspective

- Inappropriate attendees in the room (discussion complicated by need to backtrack and explain things)

- Weak facilitator (discussion often veers off topic)

- Dominating attendee(s) (broad input and real discussion get quashed)

- Meeting length inappropriate (too long or too short for the purpose)

- Venue inappropriate for the group size (some can't see or hear; uncomfortable for other reasons, and participation suffers in an effort to "get it over with")

- Venue inappropriate for the purpose (in formal venues, some attendees hesitate to speak up; in casual venues, some think serious objections won't be taken seriously; attendees may feel "obligated" in a "host" environment)

Once again, strategic thinking prior to a meeting often determines the meeting's success or failure concerning controversial or sensitive issues. Ask yourself the following key questions as you plan.

> As with race cars, **what's "under the hood"** drives a meeting's **overall success**.

SHOULD YOU FACILITATE THE MEETING?

A facilitator should know how to make key decisions about logistics (venue, timing, duration, agenda, A-V support, confirmations, cancellations), structure, group dynamics, and problem participants.

Do you know how to prevent the above time wasters? If not, you definitely need a facilitator who does. And even if you're an excellent facilitator, there are other reasons for choosing someone else to lead your meetings: 1) to allow you to participate as a team member rather than an objective facilitator; 2) to handle problem participants; 3) to bring an outside perspective on a controversial topic; and 4) to avoid the appearance of a "control-and-command" discussion and decision.

Arrange for an internal facilitator by offering to return the favor to facilitate for a colleague on another occasion. Or consider asking a skilled internal facilitator who enjoys the task and wants the visibility with higher-ups in the meeting. Although outside facilitators will expect to be paid, these professionals definitely add value in running an efficient meeting—particularly when you expect controversy, have problem participants, or face a lengthy agenda of strategic importance.

WHO SHOULD AND SHOULD *NOT* ATTEND?

Ask yourself who must sign off on key decisions. Who has veto power? Who has crucial input? Who can be a real champion for your cause in the rest of the organization? Whose support must you have if the project gets off the ground? Who are the naysayers who can doom your decision or work if their voices aren't heard?

Who should *not* attend? Who will only complicate the process and discussion? Who will likely sidetrack the meeting onto personal agendas unrelated to the project or decision? If someone you invite can't attend, do you want to *allow* them to send a representative—or maybe *encourage* them to send a representative? Think it over—before the meeting, not after the person shows up and complicates your meeting. State your "druthers" in the invitation.

WHAT'S THE *PERMANENT* SYSTEM TO CONFIRM OR CANCEL?

If you're making a list and checking it twice, you'll soon find out who's naughty and nice. No need to wait for Santa. Double-check that list of time wasters above. How often have you arrived at a meeting only to discover that a key decision maker has canceled at the last minute—and made the entire meeting useless for everyone else? Or if you've hosted a meeting, have you invited attendees and failed to receive confirmations from some invitees until start time when they appeared at the door or called in to the conference line?

A system for emergency cancellations helps prevent those unpleasant surprises. So does building a culture in which all know *and agree* that commitments and proper cancellations show respect and protect everyone's time.

Set up a system and a deadline by which all team members agree to either confirm or cancel attendance in advance. Agree that if all have not checked in to either confirm or cancel by this drop-dead deadline, the entire meeting will be canceled on their behalf. After a few such cancellations, peer pressure will remind slow or delinquent members to make a commitment for the sake of everyone's time and schedule. (Of course, as meeting leader, you can always look at the list to see who has confirmed or canceled, make the decision to cancel the meeting, and send out a cancellation notice.)

As the communicator whose reputation rests on the meeting results, *you* have to determine the meeting strategy that marks the difference between frustration and success.

CHAPTER 35

Meet Like You Mean Business

You will never see eye-to-eye
if you never meet face-to-face.

—WARREN BUFFETT,
BUSINESSMAN, INVESTOR,
AND PHILANTHROPIST

When you attend a meeting as a participant rather than as a facilitator, you produce value by contributing to the outcome—not simply by your presence. Although that may sound obvious, it's not: I've sat through meetings in which a few attendees played with their devices, worked on other projects, or left the room repeatedly to take other calls.

Such behavior is a mistake. **If you show up physically, be present mentally.** If the meeting leader fails to facilitate, understand the meeting process and follow the flow well enough so that you can step into the gap and demonstrate your leadership skills as you guide a productive discussion. Of course, don't make a big play to "take over" the facilitator role. But as a meeting participant, you can do much to steer the discussion by being familiar with meeting processes: brainstorming alternatives, analyzing potential solutions, building consensus, deciding, summarizing, transitioning to new topics, and so forth.

The meeting communication roles and strategies that follow increase your chances to end with results, not excuses because you weren't *the* leader in charge.

REIN IN A RAMBLING DISCUSSION

As Charles Kettering, the famed inventor and head of research for General Motors, once stated, "A problem well stated is a problem half-solved." As a strong meeting contributor, reel in an unwieldy discussion to respond to the question before the group. If no clear question or well-defined problem has been posed, consider that your challenge: State it succinctly for the group's focus.

ANALYZE WHERE THE DISCUSSION NEEDS TO GO

You have many choices to structure your discussion: From status quo to goal. From problem to solution. From need to criteria to options to decision. From pro/con analysis of options to decision. From opportunity to creation of new ideas to decisive action. If the meeting leader lags behind, you can suggest a structure for the group to follow. Most inexperienced facilitators will gladly allow you to help move the discussion along as opposed to drifting uncomfortably in a free-for-all situation.

If you **show up** physically, **be present** mentally.

DECIDE WHEN TO OFFER YOUR OPINION FIRST

If you intend to move ahead with your idea but want input or validation, don't set yourself up to be shot down with statements like: "I plan to do X next quarter. Anybody have a problem with that?" Or: "I'm going to be changing the policy on X to allow Y. Everybody okay with that?" Such phrasing makes some people uncomfortable. They'll need chutzpah to raise an objection or give negative feedback in front of a group—especially when the statements sound as if the decision has already been made.

Rephrase to get candid feedback: "I plan to do X next quarter. What challenges and obstacles do you think I need to prepare for?" Or: "I'm *thinking* about changing the policy on X to allow Y. I know everyone won't agree. What pushback do you anticipate I'll get?" This last rewording sounds particularly open, as if you're waiting for input before making a final decision.

Understand also that this phrasing communicates your strong opinion and that you are conceding little or no decision authority to the group. If that's your intent, let the group know that at the beginning rather than mislead them about their input on the issue.

DECIDE WHEN TO OFFER YOUR OPINION LAST

If your group includes members who seem timid about expressing themselves on controversial issues, you may want to offer your comments last. Toss out an open-ended question on your topic. Ask follow-up questions. Allow plenty of silence after people answer your questions or give input. People tend to fill silence with more information. (I've found this technique invaluable in interviewing job applicants. An original 20-second answer can turn into a valuable five-minute disclosure.)

If you'd like to share your own input about a topic, you can always do that after others have voiced theirs.

CREATE A SAFE ENVIRONMENT

In an ideal world, all meeting attendees would play nice. They would arrive on time, put away their devices, tune in to the discussion, contribute passionately, listen to their colleagues' opinions, understand the logical flow of the commentary, resolve conflict amicably, leave fully committed to the group's decisions, and be accountable for any assigned follow-up action.

But meetings may unfold similar to encounters on the playground: Passive and dominating attendees annoy each other and complicate the process. So why not simply let the passives fade into the woodwork and let the dominators take over the game board? Several reasons:

- Dominators answer every question before others have time to respond to the challenge, analyze issues, and think for themselves.

- Dominators often ramble and repeat themselves, creating boredom and impatience among the group members.

- Dominators monopolize and prevent other ideas and solutions from surfacing.

- The biased opinion of one or two dominant personalities may not represent the group as a whole, and, as a result, decisions and actions may not accurately reflect the group's thinking—or yours.

- Passives frequently complain later that they've had no opportunity for input.

- Passives often fail to engage and lend their support to important initiatives.

- Passives deprive others of their expertise.

So what's your role as a participant? You serve in much the same capacity as a panelist at a forum or industry conference. Your goal, along with that of the facilitator, is to create an environment in which everyone has a chance to contribute. That often means putting some controls on the dominator. You can:

Accept comments from the dominator without yielding the floor.
Giving verbal pats on the back typically encourages the person to keep talking and explaining. (Examples of verbal pats on the back: "That's

an idea. Others?" "Good idea." "I like that." "That could work.") *Withholding such pats* can extinguish the dominator's input.

Acknowledge a contribution with body language only—eye contact, a smile, a nod, an open palm—and then turn to someone else for another contribution.

Call on others by name to jump into the discussion: "Jaime, what do you think about X?"

Play traffic cop with a verbal cue: "Let's hear from several people on this issue." "Somebody from Legal—what do you think about the proposed change?" Or: "I'd like to hear everyone weigh in on this issue. What do the rest of you think?"

Play traffic cop with your body language or voice. Simply break eye contact, and divert attention elsewhere in the room. If on a teleconference, break the dominator's train of thought during a long ramble by asking a question: "Julie, excuse me for interrupting here. Let me ask you a question about what you just said." Then ask a short-answer question. That distraction typically breaks the ramble and gives you opportunity to regain the floor after the person's short answer.

Call the dominator by name: "Tyler, before we get on another track here, I'd like us to spend more time discussing how to..." Calling a person's name puts him or her on the spot in a gentle way to relinquish the floor—and refocuses discussion quickly to avoid embarrassing anyone.

To sum up: Being a meeting participant dropout and playing word games on your smartphone or responding to email is not the answer to meaningless meetings. Instead, contribute value by paying attention to process and rescuing an inept facilitator. Counter group-think and create a level playing field for all to participate productively. Real leaders take the initiative when the stakes are high.

CHAPTER 36

Know Your Meeting ROI

I work hard to only attend those meetings that have strategic importance and miss all kinds of other seemingly urgent meetings.

—STEPHEN COVEY, EDUCATOR, AUTHOR, AND CONSULTANT

As the meeting leader, you'll want to know the return on your **meeting** investment. If you *own* the meeting, make sure you know **the cost** and the expected deliverables (An analysis only? A **recommendation** only? A decision? Input to pass on to another party?).

Here's how to estimate your typical meeting cost:

1. Estimate the annual salary of each meeting attendee, and compute an average annual salary for the typical attendee.

2. Compute that "average" attendee's *hourly* rate based on a 2,087-hour work-year (40-hour work week according to the US Office of Personnel).

3. Multiply that hourly cost per employee by the number of meeting attendees.

4 Multiply that hourly cost by the length of your meeting.
(If you regularly meet for one hour, multiply the hourly rate
by 1. If your group regularly meets for 90 minutes, multiply
the hourly cost by 1.5. If your meetings normally last two
hours, multiply that hourly cost by 2, and so forth.)

Example:

$ 90,000 = Average attendee's annual base salary

$ 126,000 = True total cost of "average" attendee
(multiply by 1.4 to account for base salary,
employment taxes, and benefits)

$ 60.37 = Average attendee's hourly salary

× 8   Attendees
_____

$ 482.96 = meeting cost per hour for our group

× 2 =   two-hour meeting
_____

$ 965.92 = cost of two-hour meeting
(not counting venue cost or food)

Note: If the average attendee's salary is higher or lower,
adjust the cost to estimate your own meeting cost.

With these two pieces of information (cost and deliverables), you can
make better decisions about choosing a meeting as the best method
to communicate about an issue. Of course, the
outcome may be intangible input, analysis, or
recommendations—but you certainly have a
good estimate on the value of that intangible.
At other times, that meeting may produce a
very measurable cost-saving idea or new service
concept that you can compute in exact dollars.

> If you *own* the
> meeting, make
> sure you know
> the **cost** and
> the **expected**
> **deliverables**.

Again, the goal: Know the cost of typical meetings and communicate that to your team so you—or you and your team together—can evaluate the ROI of key meetings. If you consider the value worth the cost, then move ahead with the meeting.

CONSIDER BEST PRACTICES

While I never suggest meeting just because the calendar or clock says so, team members *do* need to meet at least once a year to identify communication attitudes, habits, policies, and practices that no longer work—or no longer work as well as they should. These issues can best be handled in a real-time meeting because brainstorming together can generate much broader thinking and deeper questions that quickly become too cumbersome to handle in other ways.

For example, processes and policies may outlive their usefulness. Forms, templates, and website FAQs may contain outdated information that generates only confusion and more questions—questions that necessitate your time in responding to customers, suppliers, and co-workers.

Your social media properties, intranet, website, ezines, blogs, podcasts, and other sales and marketing collateral may not be serving your current purposes. And how about your staff meetings? All-hands meetings? Customer meetings? Supplier meetings? Evaluate all the ways you and your team interact internally and externally.

Look outside your organization as well. What's new in how your customers prefer to communicate with you? Are your competitors changing how and how quickly they communicate with their customers? Have new competitors entered the market? How will these changes likely affect what your own customers expect in the way you communicate with them in the coming year?

So much for reactionary communication.

THINK INNOVATION

In addition to what you need to update, simplify, or stop altogether, identify new opportunities and improvements.

What are your ideas for improving your organization long-term? When everyone is head-down working at their current job or project, no one has time to think about improvement. But in strategic discussions, that's the main focus: Long-term gains. Increased capacity. Improved efficiency. Bigger market share. Bigger profit margins. Better products. Improved services.

Do your communication practices contribute to reaching your big-picture goals? If so, that's strategic communication. If your communication impedes rather than improves the situation, it has become problematic, not strategic.

> If your **communication** impedes rather than improves the situation, it has become **problematic, not strategic**.

Next Steps

Would you like to go deeper on the subject? Go to www.Communi cateLikeALeaderBook.com for a downloadable PDF Discussion Guide of the principles in this book, along with other resources.

www.CommunicateLikeALeaderBook.com

Get Dianna's weekly blog mailed to your inbox by signing up at www.BooherResearch.com/blog. This ezine will provide ongoing practical tips on leadership communication, executive presence, sales communication, customer service communication, interpersonal skills, productivity, and authorship.

Notes

1   Davidson, "Hard to Find." The article cites other studies that lead to the same conclusion. A LinkedIn survey of 291 hiring managers noted that 58 percent of the managers say the lack of soft skills is limiting their company's productivity. The LinkedIn survey went on to report that the ability to communicate trumped all other skills. An academic study in 2015 from Harvard economist David Deming also found that demand has increased for workers who excel in these soft skills.

2   Harter, "Obsolete Annual Reviews."

3   Harter and Adkins, "Employees Want a Lot More From Their Managers."

4   Rath, *Strengths Finders 2.0.*

5   Schoenberger, "The Right—and Wrong—Ways to Give Employees Kudos."

6   Ibid.

7   Eichinger, "Kill Your Performance Ratings." In PricewaterhouseCoopers's Annual Global CEO Survey, only 7 percent of the CEOs felt no need to change their talent practices. Of the CEOs surveyed, 93 percent reported a need to change those practices, and obviously those "practices" include what individuals do to develop themselves and their teams.

8   Saba, Retention and Leadership Survey.

9   Ibid.

10   Campbell, "The Millennials Are Coming."

11   Lunden, "6.1B Smartphone Users Globally By 2020." The author is quoting the latest annual Mobility Report from Ericsson, which uses data gathered from approximately 100 carriers globally. The number of mobile users who never or seldom turn off their cell phones is according to a Pew Research Center 2014 survey of 3,683 online and mail respondents, which was reported in a *Wall Street Journal* article (https://si.wsj.net/public/resources/images).

12 **Nink,** "Many Employees Don't Know What's Expected of Them at Work."

13 **Groysberg,** *Chasing Stars.* Groysberg discusses the strategy of both internal and **external** networking, but he says external networking for women is especially **important** because access to internal networks is limited. Groysberg has written **extensively** on his research regarding networking and growing talent, and how **each** gender fares during career moves.

Bibliography

Bersin, Josh. "Becoming Irresistible." *Deloitte Review* 16 (2015). Accessed August 8, 2016. http://dupress.com/articles/employee-engagement-strategies/.

Booher, Dianna. *Communicate With Confidence: How to Say It Right the First Time and Every Time.* New York: McGraw-Hill, 2012.

———. *Creating Personal Presence: Look, Talk, Think, and Act Like a Leader.* San Francisco: Berrett-Koehler, 2011.

———. *E-Writing: 21st-Century Tools for Effective Communication.* New York: Simon and Schuster, 2000.

———. *Speak With Confidence: Powerful Presentations That Inform, Inspire, and Persuade.* New York: McGraw-Hill, 2003.

———. *What More Can I Say? Why Communication Fails and What to Do About It.* New York: Penguin Random House/Prentice Hall, 2015.

Campbell, Shana. "The Millennials Are Coming." *TD*, April 2016, 14.

Cialdini, Robert B., Ph.D. *Influence: The Psychology of Persuasion.* Rev. ed. New York: Harper Collins/Collins Business, 2006.

———. *Pre-Suasion: A Revolutionary Way to Influence and Persuade.* New York: Simon and Schuster, 2016.

Davidson, Kate. "Hard to Find: Workers With Good 'Soft Skills.' " *Wall Street Journal*, August 31, 2016.

Eckman, Paul. *Emotions Revealed: Recognizing Faces and Feelings to Improve Communication and Emotional Life.* New York: St. Martin's Press, 2003.

Eichinger, Robert. "Kill Your Performance Ratings." Accessed August 5, 2016. http://www.kornferry.com/consultants/Roberteichinger.

Gladwell, Malcolm. *Blink: The Power of Thinking Without Thinking.* New York: Little, Brown and Company, 2005.

Goldsmith, Marshall. *What Got You Here Won't Get You There: How Successful People Become Even More Successful.* New York: Hyperion, 2007.

Goleman, Daniel. *Leadership: The Power of Emotional Intelligence*. Florence, MA: More Than Sound, 2011.

Goman, Carol Kinsey. *The Truth About Lies in the Workplace: How to Spot Liars and What to Do About Them*. San Francisco: Berrett-Koehler, 2013.

Groysberg, Boris. *Chasing Stars: The Myth of Talent and the Portability of Performance*. New Jersey: Princeton University Press, 2012.

Harter, Jim. "Obsolete Annual Reviews: Gallup's Advice." Gallup Research, September 28, 2015.

Harter, Jim, and Amy Adkins. "Employees Want a Lot More From Their Managers." *Gallup Business Journal*. Accessed April 8, 2015. www.Gallup.com/Business Journal/182321/Employees-lot-managers.aspx.

Kouzes, James M., and Barry Z. Posner. *Credibility: How Leaders Gain and Lose It, Why People Demand It*. San Francisco: John Wiley & Sons/Jossey-Bass, 2003.

———. *Learning Leadership: The Five Fundamentals of Becoming an Exemplary Leader*. New York: Wiley, 2016.

Lunden, Ingrid. "6.1B Smartphone Users Globally By 2020, Overtaking Basic Fixed Phone Subscriptions." Accessed August 2, 2016. www.TechCrunch.com/2015/02/6.

Meister, Jeanne C., and Karie Willyerd. *The 2020 Workplace: How Innovative Companies Attract, Develop, and Keep Tomorrow's Employees Today*. New York: HarperCollins, 2010.

Nink, Marco. "Many Employees Don't Know What's Expected of Them at Work." *Gallup Business Journal*. Accessed August 5, 2016. www.Gallup.com/business journal/186164/employees-dont-know-expected-work.aspx.

Pew Research Center. 2014 American Trends Panel Survey. Accessed August 8, 2016. http://www.pewinternet.org/2014/10/22/methods-the-american-trends-panel-surveys-atp/.

PricewaterhouseCoopers. Annual Global CEO Survey. Accessed August 8, 2016. http://www.pw.com/ceosurvey.

Rath, Tom. *Strengths Finder 2.0*. New York: Gallup Press, 2007.

Saba. Retention and Leadership Survey. Conducted by Harris Poll, Harris Interactive/Nielson Study, December 2014. Accessed August 3, 2016. www.saba.com/us/press-releases/go/2015/us-workforce-expected-to-experience-massive-shift-in-2015.

Schoenberger, Chana R. "The Right—and Wrong—Ways to Give Employees Kudos." Accessed June 3, 2016. http://wsj.com/articles/the-rightand-wrongways-to-give-employees-kudos-1464660022?lesla=y.

Acknowledgments

As with each book that has gone before, writing is rarely an individual project. My keynotes, consulting work, coaching, and books build on decades of prior research by teams of dedicated psychologists and social scientists, client assignments, cooperation by sponsor organizations, and hours of personal interviews with senior executives at client firms willing to share their experiences and expertise.

Specifically, I would like to thank Steve Piersanti and Neal Maillet at Berrett-Koehler for their vision for this book. Once again, it has been wonderful to work with the entire team at Berrett-Koehler, on everything from editorial to design, to marketing, to publicity, to sub-rights: Jeevan Sivasubramaniam, Johanna Vondeling, David Marshall, Maria Jesus Aguilo, Catherine Lengronne, Charlotte Ashlock, Michael Crowley, Kristen Frantz, Matt Fagaly, Zoe Mackey, Shabnam Banerjee-McFarland, Lasell Whipple, Christine Wilson, and so many others on the BK team. What a dedicated team of professionals to have in any writer's corner!

Thanks also to Linda Norton, Lori Ann Roth, Simon Blattner, and Wally Bock for their early review and feedback on the manuscript.

Again, a big thanks to Lori Ames and her team for their efforts in getting this book into the right hands of top influencers in the field of executive leadership.

Finally, to the colleagues, friends, and family members for their expertise and opinions in titling this book so that it connects with the intended audience, I'm indebted—as always—to so many!

Index

About the Author

Dianna Booher's life work has centered around communication in all its forms: oral, written, interpersonal, and enterprise-wide. As author of 47 books, translated into 60 foreign-language editions, she has traveled the globe, talking with clients and organizations on six continents about communication challenges they face at work and at home. Despite the cultural differences, two things remain the same: Communication is the basic business act. And communication either cements or destroys personal and work relationships.

Improving communication skills, habits, and attitudes dramatically changes life—for an individual, a family, an organization, and a nation. Dianna considers that an exciting and rewarding business and personal goal.

Based in the Dallas–Fort Worth Metroplex, her firm Booher Research Institute works with organizations to help them communicate clearly and with leaders to expand their influence by a strong executive presence. She also founded the communication training firm Booher Consultants, which provides training to corporate clients on writing, presentation skills, and interpersonal skills. Specifically, she has provided communication programs and coaching to some of the largest Fortune 500 companies and governmental agencies: IBM, Lockheed Martin, Raytheon, ExxonMobil, BP, Chevron, ConocoPhillips, Ericsson, Siemens,

Alcatel-Lucent, Brinker International, J.P. Morgan Chase, Merrill Lynch, Hallmark, Marriott, Northwestern Mutual, Principal Financial Insurance, PepsiCo, Novartis, Bayer, the US Department of the Army, the US Naval Surface Warfare Center, and NASA.

Successful Meetings magazine has named Dianna to its list of "21 Top Speakers for the 21st Century." The National Speakers Association has awarded her its highest honor: induction into the Speakers Hall of Fame. She is also listed among the "Global Gurus Top 30 Communicators."

The national media frequently interview Dianna for opinions on critical communication issues: *Good Morning America, USA Today, Forbes .com, Wall Street Journal, Fast Company, Success, Entrepreneur, Investor's Business Daily,* Fox, CNN, CNBC, Bloomberg, NPR, *The New York Times,* and *The Washington Post.*

She also blogs regularly for Huffington Post, *The CEO Magazine,* and FaithHappenings.com.

Dianna holds a master's degree in English literature from the University of Houston.

For more information about Dianna's work and her speaking engagements, visit www.BooherResearch.com.

HOW TO WORK WITH DIANNA BOOHER AND BOOHER RESEARCH

KEYNOTES AND CONSULTING

If you have any of these challenges, projects, or goals, Dianna can help:

— "Our next group of young leaders needs help to move up to the senior level—they lack executive presence."

— "Our salespeople make face-to-face presentations, and they need more polish."

— "Our proposals aren't working! We're losing business deals that should be ours."

— "We can't get our projects and budgets approved by the executive team!"

— "People say there's no communication around here, but we send them plenty of information, hold regular staff meetings, and update our intranet. So we have no idea what they mean!"

— "We get far too many customer complaints about our communication. It's costing us time and money to respond."

COACHING ON EXECUTIVE PRESENCE, SALES PRESENTATIONS, OR BOOK WRITING AND PUBLISHING

—If you'd like to increase your executive presence to move up in the organization, we will design an individual coaching program on topics to fit your needs and schedule.

—If your speakers for an upcoming meeting are experts in their field—but are not necessarily engaging speakers—we can help them shape and deliver a dynamic presentation!

—If you're an entrepreneur, CEO, consultant, or other professional wanting to establish your credentials by writing and publishing a book with a major publisher, Dianna can coach you through that process as well. Go to www.GetYourBookPublishedCoachingProgram.com

After consulting and coaching at more than one-third of the Fortune 500 organizations, Dianna has the research, expertise, and practical techniques to help you reach your goals.

FOR MORE INFORMATION
Booher Research Institute, Inc.
817-283-2333
www.BooherResearch.com
clients@BooherResearch.com
Dianna.Booher@BooherResearch.com

Please connect on your favorite
social media channels
@DiannaBooher
LinkedIn.com/In/DiannaBooher
Facebook.com/DiannaBooher
Plus.Google.com/DiannaBooher
YouTube.com/DiannaBooher
www.BooherResearch/blog

For more on this topic, go to www.CommunicateLikeALeaderBook.com
to download a Discussion Guide and other learning resources.

Another Book by Dianna Booher

Creating Personal Presence
Look, Talk, Think, and Act Like a Leader

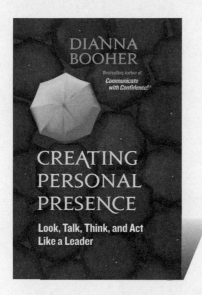

Personal presence is difficult to define but easy to recognize. People with presence carry themselves in a way that turns heads. When they talk, people listen. When they ask, people answer. When they lead, people follow. Personal presence can help you get a date, a mate, a job, or a sale. It can help you lead a meeting, a movement, or an organization. Presence is not something you're born with—anyone can learn these skills, habits, and traits. Dianna Booher shows how to master dozens of small and significant things that work together to convey presence. She details how body language, manners, and even your surroundings enhance credibility and build rapport. You'll learn to use voice and language to demonstrate competence, deliver clear and memorable messages, and master emotions. With Dianna Booher's expert, entertaining advice, you can have the same kind of influence as the most successful CEOs, celebrities, and civic leaders. Learn more at www.booherresearch.com.

Paperback, 216 pages, ISBN 978-1-60994-011-9
PDF ebook ISBN 978-1-60994-012-6
ePub ebook ISBN 978-1-60994-013-3
Digital audio ISBN 978-1-5230-8265-0

Berrett–Koehler Publishers, Inc.
www.bkconnection.com

800.929.2929

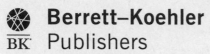

Berrett–Koehler
Publishers

Connecting people and ideas
to create a world that works for all

Dear Reader,

Thank you for picking up this book and joining our worldwide community
of Berrett-Koehler readers. We share ideas that bring positive change into
people's lives, organizations, and society.

To welcome you, we'd like to offer you a free e-book. You can pick from
among twelve of our bestselling books by entering the promotional code
BKP92E here: http://www.bkconnection.com/welcome.

When you claim your free e-book, we'll also send you a copy of our e-news-
letter, the *BK Communiqué*. Although you're free to unsubscribe, there are
many benefits to sticking around. In every issue of our newsletter you'll find

- A free e-book
- Tips from famous authors
- Discounts on spotlight titles
- Hilarious insider publishing news
- A chance to win a prize for answering a riddle

Best of all, our readers tell us, "Your newsletter is the only one I actually
read." So claim your gift today, and please stay in touch!

Sincerely,

Charlotte Ashlock
Steward of the BK Website

Questions? Comments? Contact me at bkcommunity@bkpub.com.

Certified

Corporation
bcorporation.net